Catalysts for Change

Catalysts for Change

Baby Boomers Reflect on Their Legacy to Public Education

Edited by

Frances R. Spielhagen
Paige Hendricks

ROWMAN & LITTLEFIELD
Lanham • Boulder • New York • London

Published by Rowman & Littlefield
An imprint of The Rowman & Littlefield Publishing Group, Inc.
4501 Forbes Boulevard, Suite 200, Lanham, Maryland 20706
www.rowman.com

86-90 Paul Street, London EC2A 4NE, United Kingdom

Copyright © 2024 by Frances R. Spielhagen and Paige Hendricks

All rights reserved. No part of this book may be reproduced in any form or by any electronic or mechanical means, including information storage and retrieval systems, without written permission from the publisher, except by a reviewer who may quote passages in a review.

British Library Cataloguing in Publication Information Available

Library of Congress Cataloging-in-Publication Data

Names: Spielhagen, Frances R., 1946– editor. | Hendricks, Paige, editor.
Title: Catalysts for change : baby boomers reflect on their legacy to public education / edited by Frances R. Spielhagen, Paige Hendricks.
Description: Lanham, Maryland : Rowman & Littlefield, [2024] | Includes bibliographical references. | Summary: "Catalyst for Change contains reflections of veteran educators who write about the evolution, successes and challenges, and lessons they've faced for current educators to tackle current educational challenges"— Provided by publisher.
Identifiers: LCCN 2024021788 (print) | LCCN 2024021789 (ebook) | ISBN 9781475863970 (cloth) | ISBN 9781475863987 (paperback) | ISBN 9781475863994 (epub)
Subjects: LCSH: Educational change—United States—History. | Baby boom generation—United States—Influence. | Education—United States—Social aspects—History. | Education—Standards—United States. | Education and state—United States—History. | Education and globalization—United States. | United States—History—1945–
Classification: LCC LA212 .C38 2024 (print) | LCC LA212 (ebook) | DDC 370.973—dc23/eng/20240804
LC record available at https://lccn.loc.gov/2024021788
LC ebook record available at https://lccn.loc.gov/2024021789

To my husband, Gerard Spielhagen, a fellow boomer who has traveled this five-decade road with me, and to all the boomers who have devoted their lives to public education. I also want to honor my parents, who supported my education, saying, "We work with our back, but you will work with your mind." Finally, I dedicate this to my children, Amy and Jeremy, and to their children, who will experience our legacy of change in the coming years.

Frances R. Spielhagen, PhD

*To Brayden and Brian—forever on this journey with me.
Love you both to the moon and back (and back again)!*

Paige Hendricks

Contents

Introduction: The Boomer Legacy to Education ix
Frances R. Spielhagen

Chapter 1: Urban Education: Big City versus Small City 1
Marsha Sobel

Chapter 2: The Sleeping Giant Is Awake 13
Katherine Bassett and Peggy Stewart

Chapter 3: A 60-Year Journey: A Separate and Rocky Educational Road 29
Lois Baldwin

Chapter 4: An Evolving Understanding of the Autism Spectrum: A Practitioner's Journey 55
Joanne McMahon

Chapter 5: Catalysts for Change: How Policy Changes Disrupted Inequity in STEM Access 69
Frances R. Spielhagen

Chapter 6: Gifted Education and Talent Development: Roots and Wings 85
Sally M. Reis

Chapter 7: Leadership in Times of Crisis: From First-Generation Student to College President 97
Steven DiSalvo

Chapter 8: Teacher Education Accreditation: Reflections on the Kennedy-Johnson Legacy of Institutional Reform 105
James G. Cibulka

Chapter 9: Standing on Their Shoulders: Contextual Change to Our
    Education System in the 21st Century   127
    Paige Hendricks

About the Editors and Contributors   147

Introduction

The Boomer Legacy to Education

Frances R. Spielhagen

The past six decades in U.S. history have witnessed tremendous and tumultuous changes in U.S. society. In response to the clarion call of John F. Kennedy to ask not what their country could do for them . . . (U.S. History, 1961), legions of young people in the 1960s and 1970s, the baby boomers, entered education in response to the question of what they could do for their country. This edited volume contains reflections of veteran educators who have devoted their lives to the service to others through education. They write about the changes that have evolved, their successes and challenges, and the lessons for educators now who must take this mission forward. The 60 years in question have witnessed great changes in education delivery and challenges to the concept of free public education. Those years have witnessed civil unrest, a terrorist attack on U.S. soil, an economic recession, the election of the first African American president, the growth of technology, a global pandemic, and civil unrest again.

THE BOOM YEARS: OPTIMISM AND POSSIBILITY

The years following the Second World War ushered in a time of peace and hope, prosperity, and upward mobility in the United States. Emerging victorious after a world war on two fronts, the United States welcomed home military men who settled down to make their lives in a world they had fought to create, one in which opportunity abounded for those who dared to pursue it. This optimism largely masked the racial disparities inherent in U.S. society. Those inequities would set the stage for civil unrest in the decades following

World War II, but the initial optimism of the returning soldiers and their presence back in society gave rise to an unprecedented increase in birth rates across the nation.

Birth rates "boomed" from 1946 to 1964. Marriages by U.S. soldiers during the war began the reversal of the low birthrate that had settled in during the Great Depression, but the boom took off nine months after the soldiers returned from the war. The spike in births continued for 18 years until 1964, when birth rates began to decline again. "In 1964, the 76.4 million babies born during the baby boom generation constituted a whopping 40% of the US population, which was then about 192 million" (Patterson, 1996, p. 77).

This surge in population necessarily ushered in changes in society. These changes were inevitable but not without upheaval, as diverse groups sought the fruits of freedom and optimism. In 1954, the Supreme Court ruling, Plessy versus Ferguson, stated that separate but equal school arrangements were legal in the United States. A decade later, after the assassination of Kennedy, Lyndon B. Johnson assumed the presidency and ushered in the "Great Society" amid a broiling civil rights struggle.

The first boomers came of age in 1964 and entered college in record numbers. Many of these were "first-generation" college attendees who sought careers in education as a means of leading lives of service, as the clearest path they knew and had witnessed for upward mobility, starting with their own. President Barack Obama, born in 1961, the tail end of the boom years, captured the essence of the legacy of John F. Kennedy when explaining his own life of civic engagement:

My life in many ways would not have been possible without the vision that John F. Kennedy etched into the character and hearts of America. To those of us of a certain age, the Kennedys symbolized a set of values and attitudes about civic life that made it such an attractive calling. (C-Span, May 8, 2017)

SCHOOL WAS SCHOOL: A BRIEF RETROSPECTIVE

Before World War II, citizens of the United States agreed upon a conventional concept of "school." Curriculum was standard, albeit limited, and everyone "knew" what should be taught. Adults accepted and supported the teaching of the three Rs (reading, writing, and arithmetic) as essential for functioning in society, even though only one of the three started with the letter "r." Undeterred, people in the United States thought they knew what school was about, not only what students learned but how they were supposed to learn it. Lecture and rote memorization were the predominant (only) means of instruction. Group work was rare, as was inquiry exploration, and reserved for science classes, at best. The teacher was the authority in the classroom, dispensing standard information to a select group of students.

Not everyone went to school, sometimes at all. Prior to 1950, the requirement for school attendance varied across the nation. Exit from school could occur after sixth grade, eighth grade, and for a select few, at the end of twelfth grade, with the coveted high-school diploma. Diplomas could be "general" or "academic," the latter the prequel to college attendance, reserved mostly for male students. Moreover, segregation was accepted throughout the states, so access to education varied according to race. Resources for schools serving students of color were often less adequate than for schools serving white students.

THE TIDES OF CHANGE

The brief presidency and assassination of John F. Kennedy ushered in a period of change to the status quo across the nation. Lyndon B. Johnson took the presidential helm. Almost immediately he responded to the Kennedy call for action by initiating the War on Poverty in his first inaugural address in January 1964. Civil unrest across the cities galvanized young people of all races into action. Through the Economic Opportunity Act (EOA), the Johnson administration initiated at least 40 programs targeting the poverty rate that bordered on 19% in the United States. Many of these programs focused on education as the solution to childhood poverty and the means for raising the overall standard of living for citizens in the United States.

This was the environment that fostered the initiatives of the first baby boomers, who reached age 18 in 1964. Inspired by the words of the charismatic Kennedy and empowered by Johnson's actions, these young people moved forward with optimism and purpose. Compulsory education laws were enacted across the states. Greater numbers of adults reported having a high-school diploma or general education degree (GED). The first baby boomers entered university study, many of them first-generation college goers. Those that followed stepped onto the road of optimism and opportunity that the boomers paved and a new standard understanding of what school should be.

AS THE WORLD TURNS ...

Standards-based education became the buzzword of the first two decades of the 21st century. Educators strived to address the varying needs of the diverse populations in schools. Students with special needs and those with exceptional ability tested past assumptions of a standard school curriculum.

Instead, educators created curriculum in various ways, as long as they addressed key guideposts or "standards." These standards were prescribed by the state department of education in each state, so variety was inevitable, but ultimately, all the states concurred on the basic requirements of good curriculum. Amid this sea change, professional development of the teachers was a critical component of the successful implementation of curriculum in schools.

The changing paradigm for education in the latter half of the 20th century corresponded with the changing world at large. The social and political landscape were replete with growth in interconnectedness among the nations of the world. The aftermath of World War II led to the establishment of the United Nations, with the goal of preventing future world wars. The former League of Nations, after World War I, was largely regarded as ineffective in that goal, as evidenced by the advent of the Second World War. On April 25, 1945, 50 national governments met in San Francisco for a conference and started drafting the UN Charter, which was adopted on June 25.

The isolationism of the first half of the 20th century gave way to interaction with other nations of the world. Innovations in travel and telecommunication made it possible for citizens across the globe to connect with each other. School curricula changed, as subjects such as history and geography took on new (i.e., improved) meaning. With these changes in content came changes in methods concerning curriculum, both delivery and target audience. It was not uncommon for students to interact with peers in other parts of the world, both in their own nation and internationally.

At the same time, students entering the schools brought with them individual needs and perspectives. To meet those needs, boomer educators across those decades designed programs and revised pedagogy. They incorporated new technology that seemed to arrive daily. These changes required an examination of what school means across the population. The standards movement in the early 2000s, was a wakeup call for both educators and the general population. What did it mean to be school? The chapters that follow chronicle these changes through the personal, intimate lens of contributors to this volume who have dedicated their lives to the good of the students they have served.

"ASK NOT WHAT YOUR COUNTRY CAN DO FOR YOU..."

Answering the call for service, these veteran educators effected substantial changes in the understanding and delivery of public education. Through their perspective of the changes that affected the boomer generation, each contributor to this volume describes what he or she experienced and accomplished.

Some of these accomplishments occurred on the macro level. Steven DiSalvo, president of Endicott College, recounts the path from first-generation college goer to leadership in higher education and how opportunities have been expanded over his lifetime. James Cibulka, former president of National Council for Accreditation of Teacher Education (NCATE)/Council for the Accreditation of Educator Preparation (CAEP), describes the evolution of teacher education programs and evaluation of those programs. Sally Reis, director of the center for gifted education at the University of Connecticut, discusses the rise of the theories and pedagogy for meeting the needs of highly able or gifted students. Editor/contributor Frances Spielhagen, retired teacher educator and researcher, recounts how policy changes resulted in greater STEM equity in a large southern school district.

Other changes are discussed at the micro level. Two former special educators tackle the intricacies of "special education," a term that evolved during the boomer years. Lois Baldwin chronicles the changes in the delivery of education to students with special needs, including changes in terminology and the growing understanding of "twice-exceptional students," those with exceptional intelligence and a learning disability. Joanne McMahon explains the evolving understanding of students on the autism spectrum.

Finally, three chapters address the larger issues that have arisen through the boomer legacy. Peggy Stewart, New Jersey Teacher of the Year 2005, examines the teacher leadership that emerged from all the changes; Marsha Sobel, retired school administrator, discusses the administrative challenges that school districts face to address all the myriad changes. In conclusion, Paige Hendricks, a young teacher educator, reflects on the lessons learned from the veterans.

REFERENCE

Patterson, J. (1996). *Grand Expectations: The United States, 1945–1974*. New York: Oxford University Press.

Chapter 1

Urban Education
Big City versus Small City

Marsha Sobel

Over the past five decades, urban districts have grown in scope and focus, thanks in large part to the practitioners who lived and worked in those districts. Their lived experiences and efforts have shaped the urban districts where they have devoted their professional lives. This chapter will focus on two large, urban school systems in New York State:

- New York City Public Schools, the largest school system in the country; and
- Newburgh Enlarged City School District, the largest school district located in the Mid-Hudson Valley.

Although vastly different in size, the two districts share many important characteristics. Both are very diverse in academic, racial, ethnic, and socio-economic categories but are the result of the baby boomer generation of administrators, teachers, and staff members, who sought to create equal environments for all students to learn and grow. Without these boomers in key school leadership positions, these school districts may have had very different general learning outcomes for their students.

THE NEW YORK CITY PUBLIC SCHOOLS

The New York City Board of Education was established in 1842, after the Board of Regents of the University of New York was created. By the end of the century, and after several reorganizations, a centralized Board of

Education was re-created and appointed by the mayor of the city. In 1970, decentralization created 32 elected community school boards, giving them oversight of the schools within their borders. The central Board of Education has retained some powers and is composed of two members and the mayor (Ment, 2008).

New York City's is the largest school system in the United States—more than 1.1 million students attending approximately 1,400 schools. New York City is composed of five boroughs (Manhattan, Queens, Brooklyn, the Bronx, and Staten Island) each housing multiple community-based school districts, each borough being considered a county. The diversity and size of this system is overwhelming. The state currently has 800 school districts.

The 32 community-based districts are overseen by the New York City Department of Education, with a chancellor at the head. Each district has a superintendent; and each building has a principal, as well as other administrators and teacher leaders. Each district, as well as each central office, has a number of specialized administrators to oversee the multitude of programs that the system offers its students.

Students who live in the city have many learning opportunities. They are eligible to attend schools in the district in which they live and apply to special schools in other districts throughout the system. These schools have entry requirements, including examinations to assess student competency and eligibility for their programs. Students with special needs are provided mandated services by trained and certified specialists. Dedicated schools operate for severely physically, emotionally, or academically challenged students. English Language Learners (ELLs) receive language services to enhance their learning of the English language so that they can be successful in school, in the community, and be gainfully employed.

Being part of such an expansive school system can have advantages for students as well as staff. Students can explore options for enrichment or remediation, as well as for special needs. Programs are available at all levels from elementary through high school. Specialized high schools may have auditions or admission qualifications for entry. Some of these programs are

- in many languages other than English,
- for gifted students,
- for students who have specific interests or talents, and
- for students with special needs, physical, learning, or emotional challenges.

Teachers who have specialized training in these areas are available to teach students at their level.

However, being part of such a large system can also have disadvantages. It is easy for students and staff to get lost in a system this massive. Some students are more likely to be disengaged when other students need teachers' attention, and students who disengage can easily be overlooked and "fall through the cracks." This is not to say that this will happen or that this cannot happen in a smaller setting, but the possibility of students being missed academically increases as the numbers of students increase. With so many staff members and students to oversee, one can only imagine how difficult the oversight can be.

THE NEWBURGH ENLARGED CITY SCHOOL DISTRICT

Similarly, the Newburgh Enlarged City School District (NECSD), located in the Mid-Hudson Valley approximately 60 miles from New York City, is one of the largest districts outside the city. In addition, it is one of the oldest in the state; its first public school opened in 1752. During the 19th century, many small schoolhouses were founded—some only one room—making it necessary to create school districts for oversight purposes. As the need arose, more schools were built; and in 1851 the Free School Act was passed, allowing all school-age children to attend school for free.

During the 1960s, many districts in New York State were encouraged to consolidate to provide more shared services and resources for students and be more fiscally responsible to the public. In 1963, NECSD was formed, bringing together the city of Newburgh, the town of Newburgh, the town of New Windsor, and a small portion of the town of Cornwall. Prior to this, each municipality had its own K–9 schools with students attending their own neighborhood school. The only high school, Newburgh Free Academy (NFA), held its first graduation in 1928 in the current main building. All the district's students united at NFA.

As the population of the municipalities grew, more K–9 schools were opened, and additions were put on some existing school buildings. Still, only one large high school served the entire student population.

Student demographics have changed over the years. The original schools were predominantly made up of white students. As the communities grew and the schools became more diverse, the neighborhoods remained mostly homogeneous, leading to conflict and unrest in the schools. By the 1960s and 1970s, the schools had major segregation issues with some schools being predominantly white and others predominantly black. In 1975, the Supreme Court issued a court order to desegregate the schools, setting off protests, some violent.

To integrate the schools, Newburgh developed a magnet schools' program with a variety of programs that would attract families that reflected the communities. Magnet schools are public schools that provide specialized instruction to the students (DeLolis, 2021). Developing magnet schools would allow parents to choose schools for their children. In addition, busing was offered to all students who lived more than a mile from their school.

Three magnet elementary schools were created in the first wave. One in the inner city was 98% black; one in the outlying town, 98% white. The program in the inner city was designed to attract white parents by creating a gifted and talented program. The program in the town was a fundamental program highlighting the basics. A third primary school had an ungraded program from grades K–3. These specific programs were very successful with parents, who waited in line to register their children for them. Over time, all the schools became part of the magnet school program, but the demographics of the communities changed, and the funding decreased.

Over the years, facilities have seen several reorganizations. The number of elementary schools has fluctuated; currently, it stands at nine, seven of which are K–5 and two are K–8. A full-day prekindergarten program is also housed in some elementary schools. Two middle schools house grades 6–8. Newburgh Free Academy now has a main campus with two smaller nearby campuses having specialized programs as well as core curriculum instruction.

A COMPARISON OF BOTH SCHOOL DISTRICTS

NECSD is a microcosm of the New York City schools, with many of the same characteristics, problems, and successes that NYC schools also face. Serving all their students appropriately has not been easy for either district. Some of the many hurdles have been financial challenges, staffing, changing student/family demographics, dynamic changes in educational mandates and curriculum, and evolving educator professional development.

Financial Challenges

Finances are always difficult to maintain in any organization, but it is especially trying when they depend on state or federal agencies for funding. Both school districts receive funds from both government organizations as well as additional monies from grants and local sources. Funding from the federal government comes to these districts via formulated aid. According to the National Center for Education Statistics (Brent, 2001), funding for public education in New York comes from three sources: approximately 4% from federal sources, 40% from state formula aid and grants, and 56% from local revenues. The budget for the NECSD is approximately $300 million for a little over 11,000 students and a little over 1,500 staff. The budget for the New York City school system is approximately $38 billion for about 1.1 million students and 148,000 staff members.

Both school districts require funding to provide resources for their students and salaries for staff. There are specific funding sources for districts where a large number of low-income families with children attend schools. These funds are to be used to improve students' academic achievement and ensure that students are provided with any additional services equal to other students. The school districts also seek funding for training opportunities for staff members. Curriculum materials are certainly needed for academic achievement, as well as work in the trades and arts. Funding provides the resources for the students and salaries for staff to accomplish these goals. Both school districts also have very active funded program departments that continually seek grants to provide additional academic and nonacademic opportunities and resources for students.

Larger school districts tend to have more academic programs and educational opportunities available to their students because of increased district-wide funding. Depending upon the campus, room may be available for many uniquely spaced buildings and structures in which to teach and learn. For example, art rooms are common in most of the schools in both districts and are designated for the study of art and art culture. These rooms and spaces are stocked with supplies for that purpose. Science programs can have labs retrofitted for specific areas of science. For example, biology labs can be created specifically for that subject and are complete with the appropriate equipment, materials, and supplies for students to use. Buildings that have large outdoor spaces can have fields designated for specific sports (i.e., tennis courts, swimming pools, basketball courts, football fields, etc.). Some newer buildings in both districts also provide spaces for specialized technology instruction and most buildings have school-wide networks for computer access and labs. Some of the schools in both districts that have larger funding opportunities have entire school buildings created with a theme such as theater and the performing arts. These schools offer specialized spaces for students to learn in, study, and perform for their peers and school communities.

Staffing

Staffing is always at the forefront of everyone's mind. Certified, qualified teachers must be hired in each subject and in each grade. Many specialized areas of teaching require additional skills, training, and certification. For example, students who need speech therapy need a teacher who is certified and trained in that area and is required to provide the needed services. Students who enter the country not speaking English will need language services to assist in their language acquisition of English. Teachers who are trained in ESL instruction provide those services.

In addition to the need for teachers, buildings and school districts also need certified, qualified administrators. Building principals are the primary school leaders. Their job is quite complex; and they need to be knowledgeable, compassionate, and strong. They supervise the staff, set the tone for the building, work with families on a building level, and are the liaison between their building and the central administration of the district. These qualities are all needed and hopefully found in a trained individual.

Due to the massive size of the New York City school system, it is difficult to keep all the teaching, academic support staff, and administrative positions filled. The same goes for many school districts, such as Newburgh. Staffing the requisite educational positions in each school district is an ongoing challenge and one often discussed at school board meetings and within school communities.

Changing Demographics

The populations in these large districts are not static . . . they are very fluid. People move in and out of school district locales all the time. In many cases, groups of immigrants want to find a home in a large city in which they can find work, a home that is affordable, a church in which to worship, and people of similar cultures, viewpoints, and values. As stated before, public schools are for all students in their school district, so the district must find the necessary resources (teachers, curriculum materials, etc.) to accommodate their students' needs. With this in mind, the school district needs to hire the teachers, purchase the materials, make sure the school building has room for the students, and find whatever resources are needed to meet the demands of the new members of their communities. For either district this task is daunting.

With changing demographics of students attending public schools come constant changing transportation needs. In some districts, such as Newburgh, students are provided with transportation to and from school even if the students' school (by choice) is outside their immediate community. Ideally, the transportation route must be succinct so that the ride to school is a short run and the student does not spend too much time on the bus. Commonly, if a student lives within a mile of the school, transportation is not provided. In New York City, only a small portion of students are bused to and from school; many can walk or take public transportation. These students are given metro cards issued by the department of education for use on city buses or subways.

Changing student demographics also pose challenges for both large and small school districts to successfully build rapport with their student and family communities. The smaller the school district, the more personal the attention the student may receive. Districts that only have a few hundred, or even a few thousand, students are better able to know the students and their families, as well as their teachers and staff members. In addition, teachers and staff members are more likely to know the families and each other, making it more comfortable for teachers, staff, and students to function at high levels and be successful each school day.

The larger the school district, often the more difficult it is for all members to get to know each other. In a community divided into districts such as New York City schools, it is more possible for students to know each other and their families because the districts act like smaller communities. However, the whole school system is too massive for people from one end of the system to know people at the other end. In Newburgh, though it is a large district, many events bring people from all over the district together. Further, the fact that students there can be bused to any school in the school district also promotes more familiarity of individuals across the district. It is sometimes more difficult for Newburgh neighborhood schools to build community because the students may attend a school farther from their homes, families, and neighborhoods. Therefore, the system relies upon school-based events to build community within the school buildings.

Dynamic Changes in Educational Mandates and Curriculum

New and usually unfunded innovations in education and districts are mandated to comply with these new directives. These dynamic changes in curriculum due to revised education mandates by the state education department often cost more money. District-wide teacher training must take place for the teachers to know what and how to teach their students. In addition, new textbooks, digital curriculum materials, and other resources must be provided for the teachers as well as the students when mandates change. In large districts, such as the ones we are looking at here, the cost of these changes in education mandates and curriculum are massive. For example, New York City spends $28,000 per student for materials for the 1.1 million students annually. Newburgh spends just under $27,000 per student for its 12,000 students for curriculum materials. These figures can change as both enrollment and the cost of materials changes.

Evolving Educator Professional Development

Professional development for staff is another line item in the budget and a constantly evolving area of educational practice. Staff must be informed of and trained on changes in the curriculum so they can use that "new" material or method to continue to teach their students. Depending on the scope of the topic, this professional development can take many different forms:

- *Professional development days and workshops led by teacher leaders, district administrators, or consultants hired for this purpose.* The aforementioned school districts designate several days during the school year for formal staff training and professional development. When the school district calendars are created, these professional development days are built in so that parents will know in advance that their children will not have school on those days. Professional development can be held during the school day and facilitated by district personnel (i.e., district teacher specialists or administrators) who are considered experts in specific educational fields. Frequently, outside consultants can be brought into the school district to provide professional development training. However, hiring an external expert consultant to provide training to teachers and staff is welcome but can be costly. Alternatively, workshops can be held locally or virtually by colleagues to provide new information or a refresher class on a topic already being implemented. Allowing colleagues to teach these professional development days and workshops is prudent because many educators can be considered experts in their own fields, and these individuals are easier on the school district's budget.
- *In-service classes held either online or in person after school hours.* Teachers must fulfill a number of credit hours to maintain their state teaching certification. In-service classes in New York are offered through teacher centers, colleges, or Board of Cooperative Educational Service (BOCES) Centers with the approval of the district's office of Curriculum and Instruction. These professional development classes are offered online and/or in person after school hours on various topics. Some districts offer financial incentives to encourage staff to take in-service courses and increase their educational training.
- *Classes offered by educational institutions.* In New York, local colleges or community colleges also offer education classes for teachers and staff. These classes have a cost but are needed for advanced permanent certification in a variety of areas within the field of education.
- *Teacher and staff study groups.* Teachers with common interests on specific educational topics can form study groups that meet at the

convenience of the group. These study groups can meet during the day if there is an agreeable common time without infringing on teaching time. Teachers and staff could choose to do a book study, work together on troubleshooting subjects that they deem necessary but challenging (such as a difficult topic to teach), or discuss how to best help struggling students.

The political atmosphere and policy issues also play a part in the world of education and can dictate the educational topics that are taught in professional development opportunities. Nationally, each school district has a board of elected members to oversee the policies of their district and advocate for the students. Each year, school board elections often see new board members voted in and some incumbents voted out. These changes in personnel can also change the tenor of the overall school board culture and what topics are deemed necessary and appropriate for ongoing professional development topics.

In New York City, school boards are run a little differently. Some 32 education councils each have 11 members, 2 appointed by borough presidents and the other 9 elected by parent groups. Newburgh has 9 school board members; each year, 3 members are elected by public vote the same day as the district's budget vote is held. In both cases, school boards are composed of community members who, first and foremost, answer to the public individuals they serve.

CONCLUSION

In summary, both large districts have much to offer families that live within their borders. Those families who live in New York City are used to the hustle and bustle of big city life. They think nothing of hopping on a bus or subway to get to their destination—even to go to school. They are used to having cultural, retail, and academic resources at their fingertips. And many of the city schools reflect this mentality.

Some people move out of the city for a quieter life in the suburbs. The Mid-Hudson valley location for Newburgh Enlarged City School District is just far enough out of the city for people to find this quieter life along with many of the same school and academic opportunities as the big city. The baby boomer generation of administrators, teachers, and staff who have shaped these school districts into what they are today should be commended. Many students in both districts are afforded rich academic opportunities and a variety of school choices to become equipped to successfully enter our ever-changing world.

At times, controversy has plagued both school districts. However, both still manage to be leaders in providing their students with innovative, new ways to learn. Although technology has changed the way students learn and understand academic content, basic academic skills and content areas have not changed much over time. Students still need basic skills to read (phonics, phonemic awareness, vocabulary, fluency, and reading comprehension), write (punctuation, grammar, correct spelling, clear handwriting [or keyboard skills], and sentence structure), and do mathematics (addition, subtraction, multiplication, division, fractions/decimals, percentages, visual representation, and solving for the unknown). Even with the increase in technology as a tool for learning, both school districts seek to ensure that teachers and staff have the necessary skills to instruct their students well. This goal includes having specialists in each school to assist teachers and students with resources and learning opportunities. The foundation of public education is to provide quality instruction to all students. This is not an easy task, no matter the size of the school district.

Baby boomers shaped education systems like those in New York City and Newburgh from the backbones of their ancestors and the communities their families had created. As the years unfold and communities evolve, the institutions are molded to meet the needs of their constituents. Education facilities such as one-room, multigrade schoolhouses have progressed into multilevel, multi-classroom facilities furnished with technology as well as other education resources. Baby boomers used their learned sense of culture, community, and family to create structurally sound educational institutions for their children and future generations. Despite financial challenges, constant school staffing concerns, changing community demographics, and dynamic changes in education mandates and curriculum, these boomers educated their youth using tools and techniques of the time. But the true strength of both school systems lies in the boomers' ability to adapt and alter their teaching methods and practices to change with the times and their constituents.

As the baby boomers age and retire from education, they can be proud of the legacy they leave behind. Both school systems have been lucky enough to have top-notch administrators, teachers, and staff who have worked hard to meet the academic needs of their students. Most students have fond memories of school personnel that they carry with them well into adulthood. These professionals entered the education field to make a difference in children's lives and have stayed for decades to make their mark for a future generation of students.

REFERENCES

Brent, B. O. (2001). *Public school finance programs of the United States and Canada: 1998–1999.* https://nces.ed.gov/edfin/pdf/StFinance/NewYork.pdf

DeLollis, B. (2021). *What is a magnet school?* https://www.usnews.com/education/k12/articles/what-is-a-magnet-school

Ment, D. M. (2008). Municipal Archives New York City Department of Records. In *Guide to the records of the New York City board of education* (pp. 1–166). New York City Board of Education.

Chapter 2

The Sleeping Giant Is Awake

Katherine Bassett and Peggy Stewart

> At the end of her tenure as her state's State Teacher of the Year, her superintendent entered her classroom and told her that she would not be receiving any more professional learning days to participate in the state or national projects in which she was involved, because she had received "enough" professional development as a State Teacher of the Year. She left the teaching profession within a year. (teacher leader 1, private interview, July 2022)

In their book *Awakening the Sleeping Giant: Helping Teachers Develop as Leaders*, Katzenmeyer and Moller (2001) state, "Within every school there is a sleeping giant of teacher leadership, which can be a strong catalyst for making change" (p. 2). With the advent of the teacher leader model standards (TLMS) establishing a framework for teacher leadership, that giant has awakened. The standards provide a structure and clarify expectations and roles for teacher leaders to lead from the classroom. Some states have developed teacher leadership policies, programs, and guidance based on the standards. Many districts are intentionally and purposefully growing teacher leaders, grounded in the language of the standards, within their schools. And many teachers are embracing teacher leadership professional learning and seeking opportunities to lead.

But has awakening the giant brought about the hoped-for catalyst for making significant changes in education? This chapter explores the need for teacher leadership, offers insight into the development of the TLMS, and shares discussion with individual educators on the role of teacher leadership in transforming the profession.

WHY TEACHER LEADERSHIP?

The most cogent reason for teacher leadership is, quite simply, retention, retention, retention. Many renowned researchers have cited a lack of respect and opportunity to advance in the profession as key reasons why teachers leave.

In their report *The Irreplaceables*, the New Teacher Project (2012) examined the top 20% of teachers as identified by their school data. They found that in too many cases, these teachers did not stay in teaching. And it would take between 6 and 11 potential replacements to find another teacher of their caliber. Why do they leave? Top reasons cited are lack of feedback and interest in teacher growth by administration, lack of recognition of their excellence, and lack of teacher leader opportunities.

Research conducted by Ingersoll and Smith (2003) and Johnson, Berg, and Donaldson (2005) noted that two reasons good teachers are not being retained in larger numbers are feelings of being undervalued as professionals and a lack of career advancement opportunities without leaving the classroom. Ingersoll and Smith (2003) cite that pursuit of another job and dissatisfaction combine to represent the reasons that two-thirds of beginning teachers leave the profession. In a 2013 article for *The Atlantic*, Ingersoll noted that feeling a lack of respect is a key determiner in teachers leaving the classroom.

A former state education agency leader interviewed by Bassett and Stewart (agency leader 1, private interview, August 12, 2022) whose state became an exemplar in defining teacher leadership and expanding leadership opportunities shared, "I always had a focus on teacher retention. A primary reason we lose teachers is that it's a flat profession. You can substantively grow by leaving the classroom." This held true of another award-winning educator interviewed who stated that he had been teaching math for 10 years and was seeking something more. But it became clear that the only pathway open to him was to become an administrator. He ultimately decided to leave the school setting and pursue opportunities to consult, speak, and offer professional learning (teacher leader 2, private interview, August 22, 2022).

Another significant reason teachers leave the classroom is that they do not have enough control over the school environment, classroom practices, or decision-making process. This sentiment was shared by many of the teacher leaders Bassett and Stewart interviewed (private interviews throughout August 2022). As U.S. Secretary of Education Arne Duncan noted, "Teacher leadership means having a voice in the policies and decisions that affect your students, your daily work, and the shape of your profession" (2015). A teacher from Arizona discussed the importance of teacher voice, noting,

I now advocate for my students in the local community and at the State level. People tapped me for advocacy work at the national level. I now do that for others. I feel like I have the voice now to tap others to share their voice. (teacher leader 6, private interview, August 16, 2022)

Clearly, teachers are hungry for leadership roles beyond the walls of their classrooms. Hand in hand with these roles is the need for a distributed or shared leadership model in our schools. When Bassett and Stewart present on teacher leadership, they often show a graphic of four organizational leadership systems and ask participants which model best fits their school structure. Ten years ago, virtually no one in the dozens of sessions conducted selected the distributed leadership model. Instead, participants most often selected a traditional hierarchical structure. Yet, the role of the principal is increasingly one that is overloaded and virtually impossible to perform without distributing leadership to others. Despite this, most principals are not trained how to distribute or share leadership. One principal interviewed noted that he started to realize that if he could take the leadership skill sets that teachers use with their students every day and get teachers to apply them to how we run schools, educators would be in a much better situation.

A former teacher leader, now serving as an agency director, described a unique approach to addressing teacher retention, teacher voice, and shared leadership (agency leader 2, private interview, August 12, 2022):

For me, the TLMS really changed the trajectory of what teacher leadership could be within my agency. We embarked on working with the TLMS and really got leaders to see what teacher leadership could be in the organization. What it could become. Everyone in our agency knows what it is now and they utilize teacher leaders in every aspect of work they are trying to push forward. This is largely because in 2019, I was able to get the TLMS adopted by our agency. And, people understand that those standards are synonymous with how they could build capacity for those folks who didn't want to leave the classroom but could lead from the classroom. (agency leader 2, private interview, August 12, 2022)

Identifying teacher leader roles presents some challenges, however. Traditionally, teachers have worked within the classroom setting and did not have much voice, if any, in school-wide decisions. Creating new roles and pathways for teacher voice must be done with full transparency. In their research paper for the Educational Testing Service (ETS), Jackson, Burrus, Bassett, and Roberts (2010) note that having full transparency in how teacher leaders are selected and moving away from what researcher Mark Smylie (1990) refers to as the "anoint and appoint" model of teacher leadership, is key to the success of teacher leadership in schools.

In their study on transformation in schools, including roles for teacher leaders, Laine, Coggshall, and Lasagna (2009) state, "the structural transformation of schools will necessitate a rethinking of each of the variables in the teacher career continuum and a revisualization of multiple career continua for different kinds of teachers" (p. 2).

A former state education agency official, who also served as a teacher, principal, and superintendent (agency leader 1, private interview, August 18, 2022), said,

> It became obvious that in order to sustain meaningful, serious change, it had to be embedded in the teachers. Principals don't often stay (as a general rule) as long as teachers. To sustain change it needs to be embedded in the instructional staff. It also became very evident that many instructional decisions needed to be grounded in instructional teachers. Often principals don't have expertise in all of the content areas and instructional decisions need to be grounded at the teacher level. (agency leader 1, private interview, August 18, 2022)

Shared leadership and expanding roles for teachers to lead can bring significant change to schools and to the profession. He noted, "I don't care how good the principal is. I don't care how good the superintendent is. The job is bigger than them. It needs teamwork, a partnership with teachers, not a sole decider. Power shared is not power lost; it is power multiplied" (agency leader 1, private interview, August 18, 2022).

State agencies and districts around the nation have used various approaches to address teacher leadership and retention. A district superintendent from Iowa describes a big, new undertaking (superintendent, private interview, August 19, 2022):

> The "why" for us in Iowa, is that in the 2013 Legislative Session a major bill was passed—the Iowa Teacher Leadership and Compensation system. It was a three-year roll out.
>
> About one-third of the districts came on board the first year with funding; the second year another cohort joined, again, with funding; and by year three, all Iowa schools were participating in this initiative. My district was an early adopter. (superintendent, private interview August 19, 2022)

He continues:

> A district I worked at prior to working for the state had instructional coaches in place. I didn't originally see the benefit of that. I thought it was fluff and quickly found out that these teacher leaders/coaches were some of the hardest working people in the district and offered a great level of support for all of our teachers and, specifically for some of our new to the profession teachers and those just struggling in the classroom. I had seen this in a previous district and saw how

powerful it was if you could have the resources to put such models in place. (superintendent, private interview, August 19, 2022)

A teacher from this Iowa district shared:

I was part of the grant writing process. School districts had to write a grant and the unique thing about the teacher leadership process in Iowa is it gives autonomy to districts to best meet their needs and the needs of their students. (teacher leader 3, private interview, August 19, 2022)

She continues:

We give teachers pathways into leadership: those who didn't want to go into administration but had a specific skill set and wanted to stay closer to the classroom that would benefit colleagues and benefit students. That's a big "why" behind the compensation system in Iowa. We had teachers in leadership positions. I was a curriculum leader at elementary level for a lot of years prior to the Teacher Leader compensation system. This was a way to ramp that up a little bit. We had additional monies that the state allocated to our school district and we were able to formally identify the layers of support that our students and teachers needed. Instructional coaches, lead learners (lead PLC and curriculum and instruction), and peer mentoring and induction, which is a huge component in our system. We also have Lighthouse Facilitators which help the leader-in-me work in those buildings. (teacher leader 3, private interview, August 19, 2022)

In reading reports and listening to these interviews, the key message that comes through as to the "why" of teacher leadership is increased retention of teachers, as well as lessening the load on building leaders, potentially leading them to stay.

DEVELOPING THE TEACHER LEADER MODEL STANDARDS

In the mid-2000s, realizing that teacher retention was a significant issue and becoming more so each year, the Educational Testing Service (ETS) decided to conduct research into why teachers were leaving the profession and what could reverse this negative trend. In 2008, members of ETS brought together a group of practitioners, researchers, representatives of institutions of higher education, and state education agency high-level staff to spend six months exploring the potential for roles for teachers who could lead from the classroom.

Beginning with existing research, models, and the few sets of standards, as well as a scan of teacher leadership in other countries, the Teacher Leader Exploratory Consortium (the Consortium, 2011) spent six months examining possibilities for teacher leadership. Under the leadership of Bassett and Greg Vafis, ETS employees, the consortium used an ETS-developed methodology called evidence-centered design (ECD) to unpack the characteristics of great teachers and potential teacher leaders. The collective group then cross-mapped these characteristics, looking for differentiators—what made teacher leaders differ from great teachers. Another important topic that remained throughout the development of the model standards was that of informal and formal roles for teacher leaders.

At the end of six months, the consortium determined that without standards, teacher leadership was doomed to fail. They expanded their group to focus on developing standards for teacher leadership, using the differentiators identified as a starting place. The full list of consortium members can be found in appendix A. They represent teacher leaders, principals, superintendents, national organizations, independent researchers, institutions of higher education, and state education agencies—more than 30 individuals in total. In addition, the consortium benefited from the expertise of Linda Darling-Hammond, Margaret Gaston, Mark Smylie, and Jennifer York-Barr, experts to whom the consortium could take ideas and questions.

Using the identified differentiators and an extensive list of published research on t retention and teacher leadership, the consortium worked for eighteen months to develop a first iteration of the teacher leader standards. From the differentiators captured, the consortium identified three overarching differences between great teachers and teacher leaders, and three buckets of differences, which they called shifts, that great teachers need to make to serve as teacher leaders.

The overarching differences included:
- Their students were now adults,
- They think in terms of "we," not "I," and
- They facilitate rather than directly instruct.

The three buckets of shifts included instructional shifts, policy shifts, and advocacy shifts. These shifts represent new skills that a teacher leader can acquire; they do not leave behind the characteristics that they learned as great teachers, but they take these characteristics with them and build additional skills as teacher leaders.

Because the consortium was immersed in new territory and many of the ideas discussed were not part of a traditional, hierarchical school setting, it's not surprising that many concerns surfaced as the work progressed. Among the key issues that emerged were: How would teacher leaders be licensed? Be prepared? Be paid? Where would these things fall in a state education agency? Should there be assessments for licensure?

Many of these issues were placed in a parking lot for the later writing of a policy document, such as policy issues that states would have to resolve to have a meaningful model of teacher leadership in place. These issues were outside the purview of developing standards but definitely needed to be raised. A full listing of these topics can be found in the policy document that is part of the TLMS booklet, beginning on page 21. They include:

- Do teacher leaders need to be excellent teachers?
- Do teacher leaders need to have their "own" classroom?
- How do we grow teacher leaders?
- What professional development is needed?
- What courses are needed?
- How will different states identify teacher leaders? Use teacher leaders? Use teacher leader standards?
- Can all teachers be teacher leaders?

The consortium also struggled with the many challenges to teacher leadership and what possible solutions could be found. These challenges include:

- An egalitarian system of education that frowns upon anyone "going the extra mile" or "sticking their neck out,"
- Recognized educators feeling "all dressed up with no place to grow," and
- A lack of structure to support teacher leadership in schools.

Conversations were dynamic, and at times, feisty, but consensus was brought to each issue raised. Once an initial set of standard domains and their underlying functions was determined, the draft standards went out in March 2010 for public comment. The consortium cast a wide net, garnering more than 500 responses to the draft standards.

While this work was underway, the consortium wrote the policy document, created a glossary, and aligned the standards to the Interstate New Teacher Assessment and Support Consortium (InTASC) and Interstate School Leaders Licensure Consortium (ISLLC) standards. Those cross-mapped standards are found in the appendixes of the TLMS booklet.

The consortium members carefully studied the public comment survey findings with the help of ETS psychometricians and made significant revisions to the standards. The final first iteration standards were released in 2011 in Washington, D.C. They are provided below.

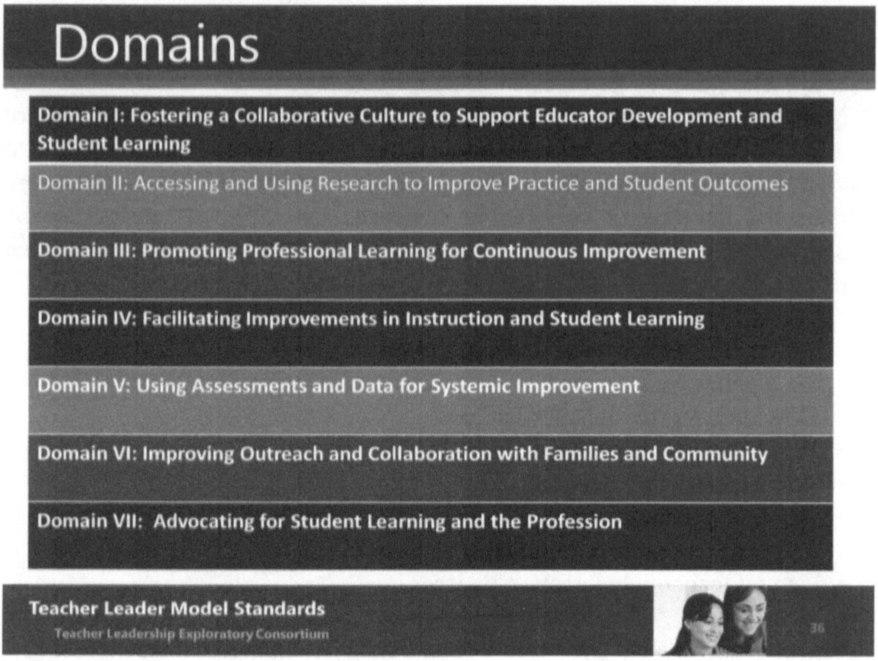

Domains

Domain I: Fostering a Collaborative Culture to Support Educator Development and Student Learning

Domain II: Accessing and Using Research to Improve Practice and Student Outcomes

Domain III: Promoting Professional Learning for Continuous Improvement

Domain IV: Facilitating Improvements in Instruction and Student Learning

Domain V: Using Assessments and Data for Systemic Improvement

Domain VI: Improving Outreach and Collaboration with Families and Community

Domain VII: Advocating for Student Learning and the Profession

Teacher Leader Model Standards
Teacher Leadership Exploratory Consortium

Figure 2.1. TMLS Domains. *Peggy Stewart.*

The standards were released to acclaim from education leaders such as Andreas Schleicher (2012), who, in his writing of *Preparing Teachers and Developing School Leaders for the 21st Century* for OECD, noted the development of the standards as a positive step. In the United States, the standards have been adopted or adapted by states, districts, and dozens of institutions of higher education. They have been used as the foundation for teacher leader certification academies in districts such as California Riverside. The standards are also being used by countries around the world.

When asked about the impact of the standards on their own teacher leadership, one teacher stated, "The standards validated that I didn't need to leave the classroom to lead, especially because I had never seen something like this in a policy document. That was exciting" (teacher leader 4, private interview, August 11, 2022). In her master's degree program, this teacher leader stated that she started her career in Domain II, using research to improve student practice. She was credentialed as an undergraduate but did not feel that her certification program at her university had been adequate. She knew she could go into a public school and be a good teacher, but she wanted to be better than that. She went to Harvard graduate school of education and did a master's degree program in teaching and learning, with a focus in science education. While there, she was on an education research team at Harvard's

Project Zero—she was in classrooms piloting instructional methods and did coding and data analysis. All her professors were in the field doing research. Thus, as a beginning teacher, she was already bringing best practices into her classroom because she had been studying and doing scientific education research.

From there, as a young teacher she provided professional learning, presented at conferences, and continued to consult with Project Zero by running small-scale research studies in her classroom. Domain III really spoke to her as a mid-career educator. By 2011 when TLMS were released, she self-identified as an advocate (Domain VII) in addition to the other two domains mentioned. Going forward, advocacy became her strength outside of her classroom walls.

This teacher leadership journey points to a key schematic of the standards: they were developed so that no teacher leader must feel that she needs to be an expert in all seven domains. Further, they were constructed so that, as a teacher leader develops, their areas of teacher leadership focus could shift. This is important, as the standards emphasize a growth mind-set as a teacher leader.

HOW SHOULD TEACHER LEADERSHIP BE IMPLEMENTED?

Is it enough to awaken a sleeping giant? What do you do with that giant once awakened? While the TLMS provide a roadmap for teacher leadership, they do not provide models to put teacher leadership in place in schools and districts. How is this being done?

Teacher Career Advancements Initiatives: Lessons Learned from Eight Case Studies, a paper developed jointly by Pearson and the National Network of State Teachers of the Year (NNSTOY; Natale, Gaddis, Bassett, & McKnight, 2016) studied eight different models of career continua in teaching. All eight models included roles for teacher leaders. Models studied revealed many common lessons learned, despite the disparity across the models. These included

- thinking strategically and proactively,
- securing broad stakeholder support and teacher voice in designing the model,
- considering long-term funding sustainability,
- considering other forms of sustainability, and
- ensuring training for principals and teacher leaders.

Every model that was studied used teacher leaders as part of their continuum of practice, although they did so in different ways. In speaking with teacher leaders in the sites studied, authors heard repeatedly that the selection process for teacher leaders needs to be completely transparent so that all educators understand how teacher leaders are selected. A second critical point from the teacher leaders involved was that piling on too many initiatives at the same time can kill a teacher leadership program quickly. They advised focusing on one thing (e.g., an adopted model of teacher leadership) and not layering things such as professional learning communities on top of that model and expecting teacher leaders to manage both programs, which may not align with one another.

In another study, *Great to Influential* (Jacques, Weber, Bosso, Olson, & Bassett, 2016), part of a three-study series by National Network of State Teachers of the Year (NNSTOY), American Institutes for Research (AIR), and other partners, authors asked participating teachers—all recognized educators—where their own teacher leadership most frequently lived and in what roles they were serving as a teacher leader. The teachers responded as noted in the chart below. This study notes that districts should consider hybrid teacher leader roles and provide guidance and models for distributed leadership. Further, it recommends increasing and improving preservice and novice educator exposure to teacher leaders.

In looking at the data presented, one can easily see the TLMS reflected in the roles these educators sought out and filled.

Speaking with two educators whose teacher leadership moved them beyond the classroom but who are still in their schools or districts was enlightening. These educators did not leave their classrooms because they were tired of teaching; they wanted to make a still larger difference. One, named his state's Teacher of the Year and then National Teacher of the Year, found that he had many avenues to teacher leadership both within and beyond his school. He eventually became an assistant principal, then principal in his own district, and is now principal of the high school in which he had taught.

When asked what role the standards played in his development as a teacher leader, he shared,

> There is the organic growth of teacher leaders, they want to get better, but sometimes they peak a little. Sometimes they can't grow more until they become intentional. They need to be more intentional. How do I intentionally grow? Improve? What are areas that I want to improve on or areas where I want to not focus on so I can be more intentional on where I want to grow? (principal, private interview, August 24, 2022)

He continued,

Improving Others' Practice

- **92%** facilitated professional development
- **83%** organized whole-school, grade-level, or team projects
- **82%** had informal leadership roles
- **80%** had formal leadership roles where they were jointly accountable for colleagues' student outcomes
- **69%** provided formal coaching or mentoring
- **59%** were observed by other teachers
- **58%** were instructional coaches or mentors
- **58%** shared research findings with colleagues
- **49%** conducted preclinical observations of student teachers
- **48%** conducted peer review evaluations

Improving Education in the District or Community

- **81%** served on school or district leadership teams
- **69%** conducted curriculum development
- **66%** developed collaborative projects with the community
- **30%** reached more students through blending learning
- **24%** reached more students by leading a teaching team

Engaging in Policy or Research

- **92%** presented at conferences or to peer groups
- **89%** served on forums, workshops, or conferences
- **85%** met with policymakers
- **75%** served on policy committees or task forces
- **33%** served as union or association leaders

Personal Advancement

- **66%** took coursework or developed knowledge in advanced pedagogy
- **53%** took coursework in teacher leadership
- **50%** conducted research
- **31%** assumed department chairmanships
- **24%** scored educator assessments

Figure 2.2. Great to Influential Study Results. *Teacher Leader Model Standards: Teacher Leadership Exploratory Consortium, ETS.org.*

That's where the TLMS comes in. It brings the intentionality and almost the cementing of the fact that we need this, need the teacher leader role. It's not a nicety. It's something we need. It's by design. The title Principal originally was the head teacher. (principal, private interview, August 24, 2022)

THE IMPACT

Since the release of the teacher leader model standards, the phrase "teacher leader" has gone from being a role one seldom heard or used to being a generally accepted role within the education ecosystem. In the United States alone, hundreds of master's and doctoral programs offer degrees in teacher leadership. A number of states have developed licensure and certification criteria for teacher leaders. Internationally, teacher leaders are equally, if not more, prevalent. And the standards are being used in countries from England to Kazakhstan.

The chapter authors asked each educator they interviewed about the perceived impact of teacher leadership on the profession, particularly on the issues that brought teacher leadership to the forefront in the first place—educator retention and greater job satisfaction, both for teachers and principals. Their thoughts are revealing.

One teacher leader interviewed, leading from outside the school as a provider of professional learning to other teachers, training teacher leaders, and giving motivational talks, says, "Reading the standards for the first time was like, whoa, it's all here. The standards brought into context what I had been trying to do. They helped me to mark my own pathway as a teacher leader" (teacher leader 2, private interview, August 22, 2022).

Another, also outside the P–12 classroom but now teaching prospective teachers as well as running a master's program in teacher leadership for a major college, shared:

> One of the cornerstones of the TLMS is that it opens up the world of teaching to be more than in your classroom. Of course, that's by design, teacher leadership. Thinking about what you do in your classroom and outside your classroom. One stuck out to me that I never thought of before. Advocacy, thinking of teachers as advocates of change and how we implement that change. That was huge for me. For my practice and how I train teachers now.
>
> In the role I'm currently in there is a course specifically dedicated to outreach and advocacy because it's so important for teachers and teacher leaders to have. Not only are you teaching kids and connecting with families and engaging with school leaders, but you are also doing advocacy work outside the school walls, including attention to policy, attention to ethics, ethical review, etc. Broadening my scope of what it means to be an educator is what the TLMS did for me. (teacher leader 5, private interview, August 15, 2022)

One of the state agency leaders interviewed stated,

> We saw with several districts that the standards, and how we implemented them, made some difference or maybe significant difference in teacher retention. Part of the Tiered Certification included an induction certification (for all 180 schools). This is probably where they had the most success (numerically). Superintendents and Principals were using their teacher leaders in the induction certificate process.
>
> Richard Ingersoll stated that we lose about 1/2 of our teachers during what we had as an induction phase (the first 5 years of teaching). Take a few percentage points off because of various different circumstances. Let's say you lose 35%

of your teachers. The dollar amount nationally (totally astounding) and the time training and recruiting, leads me to think that the induction stage is the biggest area of impact.

One of the greatest impacts that is a requirement each year is that I have to produce a report for the state for our goal areas and rate how well we feel we met our goals. The goals are very tightly aligned to the pathways (mentoring and induction, providing job embedded professional learning through instructional coaching, guaranteed viable curriculum). The one we fully met is the mentoring and induction goal. We have worked the last few years to provide different layers of support to teachers new to the profession and also to those new to our district. They each have individual peer mentors that work on the nuts and bolts, cheerleader, support, marigold for new teachers. And instructional coaches who design, particularly for first- and second-year teachers, mentoring seminars that are aligned to professional growth goals, theory and demonstration, sit and get monthly and side-by-side in classrooms with practice feedback loop. (agency leader 1, August, 18, 2022)

The superintendent added,

> The increase in retention rates for new to the profession teachers and the broad spectrum of support are impacts of the way in which we implemented the standards. In medical terms, constant monitoring of newborns (new to the profession) by instructional coaches can do this. Intensive care in the form of intensive assistance plans which teacher leaders and coaches offer is another support. An evaluator can evaluate, but coaches can support improvement in non-threatening ways. Finally, life coaching and check-ups with teacher leaders working to refine their own skills to help them support others more effectively is key. (superintendent, private interview, August 19, 2022)

With all of these from-the-field examples of the power of teacher leadership, backed by meaningful research, it is clear that teacher leadership, and the development of the teacher leadership model standards, have made a significant difference in our nation's schools, student learning, and professionalizing teaching.

In her introduction to the book, *Adventures in Teacher Leadership*, Bassett (2019) states,

> In order for teacher leadership—and our efforts to retain great teachers and principals in our profession—to succeed, we must learn from expert educators, apply the lessons they have learned, and take important next steps to change our culture. Doing so will enable teacher leadership to thrive and a true career continuum, allowing for teacher expertise to exist. (p. 4)

APPENDIX

Teacher Leadership Exploratory Consortium

Affiliation	Name
American Federation of Teachers	Rosalind LaRocque
American Institutes for Research	Molly Lasagna
Arkansas Department of Education	Beverly Williams
Bayonne Public Schools	Deborah Shine
Bethel College	Allen Jantz
Brandeis University	Vivian Troen
California Commission on Teacher Credentialing	Cheryl Hickey
Center for Teaching Quality	Barnett Berry
	Ann Byrd
Council of Chief State School Officers	Lois Adams-Rodgers
	Mary Canole
	Kathleen Paliokas
Dolphin Terrace Elementary School,	Dana Boyd*
Ysleta Independent School District, Texas	Kristen Navarro
Edgar Allan Poe Middle School, San Antonio Independent School District, Texas	Kimberly Ash
Education Commission of the States	Barbara Thompson
Educational Testing Service	Katherine Bassett*
	Gregory Vafis
Fairfax County School District, Virginia	Leslie Butz
	Jack Dale
Georgia Professional Standards Commission	Kelly Henson
	Tom Higgins
Harvard Graduate School of Education	Katherine Boles
Kansas State Department of Education	Pamela Coleman
Kentucky Education Professional Standards Board	Robert Brown
	Phillip Rogers
Learning Forward/National Staff Development Council	Joellen Killion
Malverne School District, New York	Steven Gilhuley
	Marguerite Izzo*
Montclair State University	Ada Beth Cutler
National Association of Elementary School Principals	Carol Riley
National Education Association	Linda Davin
	Segun Eubanks
New Jersey Department of Education	Eileen Aviss-Spedding
	Christopher Campisano
	Victoria Duff
Ohio Department of Education	Marilyn Troyer
Oregon Teacher Standards and Practices Commission	Keith Menk
Princeton University	Anne Catena
State of Tennessee Board of Education	David Sevier
Temple University	Heidi Ramirez
The Danielson Group	Charlotte Danielson
University of Phoenix	Meredith Curley
Vernon Township High School, New Jersey	Peggy Stewart* **
Virginia Commonwealth University	Terry Knecht Dozier ** ***
Walla Walla School District, Washington	Anne Swant**
Washington Professional Educator Standards Board	Esther Baker
	Joseph Koski
West Virginia Department of Education	Nathan Estel
	Karen Huffman
Writer/Consultant for Teacher Leadership Exploratory Consortium	Catherine Fisk Natale

* State Teacher of the Year
** National Board Certified Teacher
*** National Teacher of the Year

Figure 2.3. Teacher Leadership Exploratory Consortium. *Teacher Leader Model Standards: Teacher Leadership Exploratory Consortium, ETS.org.*

REFERENCES

Coggshall, J., Lasagna, M., & Lane, S. (2009). *Toward the structural transformation in schools: Innovations in staffing.* Chicago, IL: Learning Point Associates.

Ingersoll, R., & Smith, T. (2003). *The wrong solution to the teaching shortage.* Alexandria, VA: ASCD.

Jackson, T., Burrus, J., Bassett, K., & Roberts, R. (2010). *Teacher leadership: An assessment framework for an emerging area of professional practice.* Princeton, NJ: ETS Research Report Series. https://doi.org/10.1002/j.2333-8504.2010.tb02234.x

Jacques, C., Weber, G., Bosso, D., Olson, D., & Bassett, K. (2016). *Great to influential.* Washington, DC: Center for Great Teachers and Leaders at AIR and National Network of State Teachers of the Year.

Johnson, S. M., Berg, J. H., & Donaldson, M. L. (2005). *Who stays in teaching and why: A review of the literature on teacher retention.* Boston, MA: The Project on the Next Generation of Teachers.

Katzenmeyer, M., & Moller, G. (2001). *Awakening the sleeping giant: Helping teachers develop as leaders* (2nd edition). Thousand Oaks, CA: Corwin.

Mieliwocki, R., & Fatheree, J. (2019). *Adventures in teacher leadership: Pathways, strategies, and inspiration for every teacher.* Alexandria, VA: ASCD.

Natale, C. F., Gaddis, L., Bassett, K. & McKnight, K. (2016). *Teacher career advancement initiatives: Lessons learned from eight case studies.* Austin, TX: Pearson.

Riggs, L. (2013). *Why do teachers quit? And why do they stay? The Atlantic.*

Schleicher, A. (Ed.). (2012). *Preparing teachers and developing school leaders for the 21st century: Lessons from around the world.* Paris, France: OECD Publishing. http://dx.doi.org/10.1787/9789264xxxxxx-en

Smylie, M., & Denny, J. (1990). Teacher leadership: Tensions and ambiguities in organizational perspective. *Educational Administration Quarterly, 26*(3) 235–259.

The Teacher Leader Exploratory Consortium. (2011). *The teacher leader model standards.* https://www.education.udel.edu/wp-content/uploads/2013/07/Exploratory-Consortium.pdf

TNTP. (2012). *The irreplaceables: Understanding the real retention crisis in America's urban schools.* https://tntp.org/assets/documents/TNTP_Irreplaceables_2012.pdf

Chapter 3

A 60-Year Journey

A Separate and Rocky Educational Road

Lois Baldwin

1960S DECADE

When President John F. Kennedy, at his swearing-in ceremony, stated, "Ask not what your country can do for you, ask what you can do for your country," he could have been talking directly to the educators of students with disabilities as well as educators of gifted and talented students because there was much to do to make the significant changes needed in both fields. Educators' understanding of how to recognize, identify, and educate students with mild or moderate disabilities or cognitive gifts was imprecise or nonexistent. The 60-year journey to make improvements in both special and gifted education has been both uncertain and forward moving. This chapter will follow the progress (or lack of it) for each field. It will also show how both special and gifted and talented education came together to form a specialized entity known as twice-exceptional or "2e" education.

At the time of Kennedy's inauguration, there were numerous instances of segregation and exclusion of those individuals who were considered different due to physical, learning, and/or emotional challenges (Goddard, 1920; Meldon, 2017). Terms such as "deaf and dumb," "trainable," "mongoloid," "imbecile," and "idiot" were used frequently to describe anyone who was having difficulty learning or who learned differently. Students with special learning and/or social/emotional needs were sent away to segregated schools or facilities or stayed home and received little or no formal education.

Although the country had just gone through a terrible decade with children and adults contracting and being negatively affected by polio, no provisions were made for physically disabled individuals who needed to use crutches or wheelchairs for ambulation. It was up to the individual's family or community to find ways to assist the affected person. The documentary *Crip Camp* (Newnham & LeBrecht, 2020) illustrates the struggles of individuals with disabilities and their radical advocacy for disability rights. Crip Camp showed visuals of those who were unable to cross a street, to access public transportation, or to eat in a restaurant because they were unable to get over the curb or in a door while in a wheelchair or on crutches. This documentary brought forth "the power of accessibility for all."

Prior to Kennedy's inauguration and for many years after, parents who bore children with Down syndrome were often told to tell their families and friends that their child died at birth and to have the child committed to an institution. For example, playwright Arthur Miller and his wife, who gave birth to a Down syndrome child, ultimately had the child institutionalized. Similarly, when their son Jason was born, Emily and Charles Kingsley were told that same devastating news. The doctor told the Kingsleys that their baby boy belonged in an institution, and they should not try to see him or become attached. "He said that 'this mongoloid' would never learn to speak, think, walk, or talk" (Solomon, p. 171). Many reasoned that these special children were not considered to be truly human. The ethicist Joseph Fletcher wrote that there was "no reason to feel guilty about putting a Down's syndrome baby away, whether it's 'put away' in the sense of hidden in a sanatorium or in a more responsible lethal sense. It is sad, yes. Dreadful. But it carries no guilt. True guilt arises only from an offense against a person, and a Down's is not a person" (Bard & Fletcher, 1968, p. 64).

The Kingsleys defied the doctor and took their son home where they implemented "early intervention," a totally new concept at the time. They bathed Jason in Jell-O to give him different sensory sensations and entertained and stimulated him with mobiles, books, foreign languages, and music. These activities made such a difference that when he was six, Jason was the first such child to appear on *Sesame Street*, where he counted to ten in Spanish (Kingsley & Levitz, 2007, p. xii). Jason was able to count to ten in twelve languages, read at four years old, and could distinguish Bach from Mozart. He also graduated from high school with a diploma when no one thought that was possible.

Parents with children on the autistic spectrum and developmental delays were also feeling dismayed by the lack of services, help, and compassion. These parents found that once they could no longer handle a difficult, uncommunicative child, the recommendation was to send him to an institution. Understanding about what caused autism was limited. Psychiatrist Leo

Kanner believed that autism was due to a lack of maternal warmth. He coined the term "refrigerator mother," which added more guilt to parents, especially mothers, who were struggling with their developmentally delayed child (Solomon, 2012).

Although parents sent their handicapped children to state-run institutions with the assumption that they would be well taken care of, the institutions (such as the infamous Willowbrook State School) were exposed in the early 1970s for their neglect and terrible conditions. These facilities were woefully understaffed, and the staff too poorly trained to take care of the residents with compassion and care. When President Kennedy's brother Robert visited Willowbrook in 1965, he called it "a snake pit that needed to be overhauled" (Fisher, 1996). One sibling of a Willowbrook resident noted in the documentary *Unforgotten: Twenty-five Years After Willowbrook* that "Willowbrook was more than a place. It was an attitude of disrespect for people with handicapping conditions" (Fisher, 1996). It was not until the reporter Geraldo Rivera exposed the horrible abuse and lack of basic care of the Willowbrook residents that society demanded change and the closing of the facility.

President Kennedy was very aware of the issues that families who had children with mental retardation faced because of his intellectually challenged sister, Rosemary. In 1962, Kennedy announced that research into intellectual disability was to become a national priority and established the President's Panel on Mental Retardation (John F. Kennedy Presidential Library and Museum, n.d.). The panel's recommendation led to legislation launching the National Institute of Child Health and Human Development. President Kennedy signed a second bill in 1963 that funded the construction of facilities, including research centers and community-based centers, to research causes of intellectual disabilities and to increase the care and understanding of individuals with intellectual disabilities.

President Kennedy's sister, Eunice Kennedy Shriver, became very instrumental in helping to change attitudes of individuals with disabilities through her advocacy work. Prior to her 1962 article in the *Saturday Evening Post*, many people felt that retardation was caused by poverty and poor living conditions. She wrote and spoke about the fact that families of wealth and position also had children with mental retardation. She wanted individuals with disabilities to be integrated into society and to be seen as human beings with rights and possibilities (Shriver, 1962). Because of her advocacy work, the Special Olympics was founded with the first games happening in 1968 ("History," 2022).

During the 1950s and 1960s, all students with disabilities typically were lumped together and segregated from the rest of the school population. Although students with learning disabilities, dyslexia, ADHD, and similar conditions were not usually sent to institutions, they too felt the effects of discrimination and segregation. A gifted student with dyslexia could be sitting in class next to a child who was struggling to learn basic concepts because of an intellectual impairment. Classes with students identified as needing special education services were usually isolated in remote areas of the school such as the basement or attic. Special education students' access to mainstreamed students in the building would be limited. Students in need of special education services were rarely included in the school's activities such as lunch, recess, and assemblies; but if they were, they were seated by themselves in a corner with little or no social interaction with the general student population. Students in these "special" classes were often referred to by students in the general school population as "retards," "dummies," "idiots," or other derogatory names or terms.

GIFTED AND TALENTED PRACTICES

In the 1960s, gifted and talented education was going through its own growth and change. The launch of Sputnik by the Russians in 1957 set off the space race and a desire by the federal government to find the best and brightest among our students to help our country compete in the race to the moon. Congress swiftly passed the National Defense Education Act (NDEA) in 1958 that focused on funding higher education through increased access to student loans, increased K–12 public education reform, as well as finding and training young scientists and mathematicians ("Sputnik Spurs Passage of the National Defense Education Act," n.d.). Prior to the act, the definition and identification of giftedness was based solely on an IQ score from a single test. However, NDEA expanded the identification of gifted and talented students to include both aptitude and ability measures (Jolly & Robins, 2022). By the mid-1960s, most school districts were giving their students aptitude tests to identify their most able students and were providing more rigorous science and math courses for those students ("History of Standardized Testing in the United States," 2020).

1970S DECADE

The civil rights movement of the 1960s changed educational focus and priorities leading into the next decade. Attention to the needs of the students who were identified as gifted dwindled; with the signing of the Elementary and Secondary Education Act (ESEA, 1965), the focus and funding turned to public school integration of low-income and minority students. After Kennedy's assassination, President Johnson used the passing of ESEA as a key component to his War on Poverty. ESEA "was designed to aid low-income students and to combat racial segregation in schools" (Gamson, McDermott, & Reed, 2015) through its Title 1 component, "compensatory education" for "disadvantaged students." As a result, federal funding to support students identified as in need of special education services and those in need of gifted and talented services were targeted by other measures.

SPECIAL EDUCATION PRACTICES

The 1970s marked a significant change for students with special education needs because of major federal legislation. The landmark legislation, the Education for All Handicapped Children Act (EHA; also known as PL 94–142), was passed in 1975. EHA supported "states and localities in protecting the rights of, meeting the individual needs of, and improving the results for infants, toddlers, children, and youth with disabilities and their families" ("A History of the Individuals with Disabilities Education Act," 2022). This federal law mandated free, appropriate public education (FAPE) for all children with disabilities, introduced the concept of least restrictive environment (LRE; a principle guiding a child's special education program), and ensured due process rights for children with disabilities. In addition, PL 94–142 defined "learning disabled" as a specified category of special education for the first time and required all special education students, including those with learning disabilities, to receive an individualized education plan (IEP) to assist with their schooling. The IEP document required that schools identify goals and growth targets for the student to be tracked by a special educator on a regular basis. It also provides accommodations and modifications implemented throughout the school day to allow the student to progress academically, socially, and emotionally.

The PL 94–142 legislation was a game changer because schools were required to establish resource rooms and provide services for their learning disabled and other handicapped children. Schools scrambled to determine how to identify their learning-disabled students, how to write an IEP that focused on the child's individual learning and social/emotional needs, and how to provide the modifications and accommodations that each student needed. Although funding was never felt to be adequate, the federal government provided monies, grants, and training to help facilitate the major changes occurring in school districts due to the mandatory implementation of PL 94–142.

GIFTED AND TALENTED PRACTICES

In 1972, U.S. Senator Jacob Javits and U.S. Representative John Erlenborn cosponsored legislation that provided funding and mandates for gifted education services in public schools. At the time, Javits and Erlenborn had been working closely with the commissioner of education, Sidney Marland, and his advisory committee to determine specific types of services and programs necessary to meet the needs of gifted children. These conversations began because of the so-called Marland report, which was published in August 1971 by Sidney Marland in response to section 806 of PL 94–142. Section 806 dealt specifically with students identified in need of gifted and talented education services but provided little information about how to accomplish this massive task in public schools. In letters to the president of the Senate and speaker of the House of Representatives, Marland claimed this "painstaking study . . . confirmed our impression of inadequate provisions for these [gifted and talented] students and widespread misunderstanding about their needs. . . . The report outlines the immediate steps we are taking in response to some of the major deficiencies uncovered" (Marland, 1971). The Marland report created the first national definition of giftedness using a multidimensional description:

> Gifted and talented children are those identified by professionally qualified persons who by virtue of outstanding abilities, are capable of high performance. These are children who require differentiated educational programs and/or services beyond those normally provided by the regular school program in order to realize their contribution to self and society. (p. ix)

Further, the Marland report describes:

> Children capable of high performance include those with demonstrated achievement and/or potential ability in any of the following areas, singly or in combination:

1. general intellectual ability
2. specific academic aptitude
3. creative or productive thinking
4. leadership ability
5. visual and performing arts
6. psychomotor ability (removed in 1978; p. ix)

The Marland report determined that identification of gifted and talented students would "encompass a minimum of 3 to 5 percent of the school population," should be identified by both objective and "professional evaluation measures" by "professionally qualified persons include[ing] such individuals as teachers, administrators, school psychologists, counselors, curriculum specialists, artists, musicians, and others with special training who are also qualified to appraise pupils' special competencies" (p. ix). This information and the entire Marland report influenced the field of gifted and talented for future decades.

Although the Marland report with its definition for gifted and talented students was a huge leap for the field, it missed the mark by not insisting on federally mandated services or funding. As Jolly and Robins (2022) noted, "This missed opportunity left gifted education and gifted students vulnerable to the often-volatile nature of interest and apathy toward this particular group of students" (p. 25). Instead of financing gifted and talented education, Congress amended the Elementary and Secondary Act of 1965 with the Gifted and Talented Children's Education Act in 1978. The 1978 Act established the National/State Leadership Training Institute, which provided financial incentives through grants for states to create programs for gifted and talented children from preschool through 12th grade. It also included provisions for universities to recruit and support graduate-level students to become seminal figures in the gifted and talented field. This act and the monies eventually were repealed, only to resurface in the following decade.

Previous to the Marland report, gifted students were identified solely based upon their IQ. After its publication, more inclusive definitions and works citing more holistic ways to identify gifted and talented children emerged. Researcher and professor Abraham Tannenbaum (1983) stated,

> The movement away from exclusive reliance on IQ and its correlates to define giftedness is not intended simply to devalue the IQ. Instead, the argument is that IQ limits giftedness to traditional academics and is not helpful in distinguishing among different kinds of intellectual functioning. (p. 75)

Dr. Tannenbaum instead posited that giftedness was a five-factor "sea star" model used for identifying potentially gifted and talented children. The model's five factors include general ability, special ability, non-intellective factors, environmental factors, and chance factors. When combined, the "sea star" model created a more complex vision of individual excellence and one that allows children to be viewed in a more comprehensive manner during the identification process.

In 1978, educational psychologist and researcher Joseph Renzulli developed the three-ring conception of giftedness (Renzulli, 1978). The purpose of this model was to develop an approach to identify gifted and talented children within school environments. The three rings of the model include above-average ability, creativity, and task commitment. According to Renzulli (2022), "students who possess the combination of these three traits exhibit gifted behavior" (para. 3).

1980S DECADE

In this decade educators and researchers became curious about children and, in particular, a small yet growing number of children identified as both disabled and gifted and talented. An increased understanding of learning difficulties sparked interest in children who have both a disability and an exceptionality. This field would later emerge as a bridge between PL 94–142 and the Javits legislation.

SPECIAL EDUCATION PRACTICES

Just as in the late-1970s, school districts in the 1980s were busy implementing PL 94–142 and the increased federal guidelines that accompanied this legislation. Additional "new" guidelines were more specific about what varying disabilities looked like and what abilities identified learning disabled children were capable of achieving. The *Federal Register* (1977) guidelines identified children with learning disabilities as:

> those children who have a disorder in one or more of the basic psychological processes involved in understanding or in using language, spoken or written, which disorder may manifest itself in imperfect ability to listen, think, speak, read, write, spell, or do mathematical calculations. Such disorders include such conditions as perceptual handicaps, brain injury, minimal brain dysfunction, dyslexia, and development aphasia. Such a term does not include children who have learning problems which are primarily the result of visual, hearing, or motor handicaps, of mental retardation, of emotional disturbance, or of environmental, cultural, or economic disadvantage.
>
> A team may determine that a child has a specific learning disability if (1) the child does not achieve commensurate with his or her age and ability levels in one or more areas [seven of which are specified—oral or written expression, listening comprehension, basic reading skill or comprehension, mathematics calculation or reasoning] when provided with learning experiences appropriate for the child's age and ability levels; and (2) the team finds that a child has a severe discrepancy between achievement and intellectual ability in one or more of [these] areas. (p. 65)

This federal definition did not change the disagreement between experts, researchers, and educators about how to define children with learning disabilities or their specific disabilities or how to help them learn in schools. In 1981, the National Joint Committee for Learning Disabilities (NJCLD) and the Association for Children and Adults with Learning Disabilities (ACLD) along with other organizations[1] met to compile a definition of the term "learning disabilities." According to the NJCLD (1997), learning disabilities:

> Is a general term that refers to a heterogeneous group of disorders manifested by significant difficulties in the acquisition and use of listening, speaking, reading, writing, reasoning, or mathematical skills. (para. 2)

The NJCLD stated that these disorders may occur throughout an individual's lifetime and may occur with other disabilities (e.g., sensory impairment, mental retardation, serious emotional disturbance) but do not include "problems in self-regulatory behaviors, social perception, and social interaction" (para. 3). These notations further clarified the federal (PL 94–142) definition and sought to increase inclusion of many individuals in need of special education services for future organizations.

GIFTED AND TALENTED PRACTICES

In the early 1980s, one individual addressed intelligence and giftedness as more than a single IQ score. Howard Gardner's theory of multiple intelligence (MI) was made up of seven types of intelligence: linguistic, logical-mathematical, spatial, musical, bodily-kinesthetic, interpersonal, and intrapersonal.[2] His book, *Frames of Mind: The Theory of Multiple Intelligences* (originally published in 1983), pushed educators to teach skills and information aimed at different intelligences with the focus on students' individual MI strengths. These intelligences, as posited by Gardner, show an individual's computational power and should not be confused with learning styles, which are how an individual approaches learning in general (Strauss, 2013).

In addition, this decade's emphasis on understanding learning disabilities also influenced the field of gifted education. Educators and researchers were looking at why some gifted students were underachieving and hypothesized that they might have a learning disability or other handicapping condition. The very first book on the subject written by C. June Maker (1977), *Providing Programs for the Gifted Handicapped*, helped introduce the concept that individuals who were gifted could also be physically handicapped and/or have a disability of some kind. Further, a group of educators and researchers from Johns Hopkins University, Columbia University, and the

University of North Carolina collaborated to write *Learning-Disabled/Gifted Children: Identification and Programming* (Fox, Brody, & Tobin, 1983). Again, the concern was that educators working with students with a learning disability might overlook a student who was also gifted, or that the reverse could also be true. These publications sparked the beginning of discussions about the consequences of one condition possibly "masking" another condition and how this challenge affects the academic, social, and emotional success of gifted students who were underachieving.

Dr. Susan Baum and I cofounded the Association for the Education of Gifted Underachieving Students (AEGUS), the first national advocacy group for gifted students who were underachieving due to learning, emotional, and cultural challenges. Two goals of AEGUS were to develop an awareness of the existence and needs of identified gifted underachieving students and to create opportunities for an exchange of ideas among professionals, families, policy makers, and students concerned with the issue of underachievement (former AEGUS publication). To achieve those goals, the organization conducted conferences every year for more than 30 years in various parts of the country including New York, Oregon, Minnesota, Colorado, Alabama, Maryland, and California. For most parents and educators, the AEGUS conference was their first opportunity to interact with professionals and experts who had knowledge about causes of gifted underachievement as well as to learn about strategies that could be implemented to make these students more successful in the school environment. AEGUS is no longer in existence because other organizations now provide those opportunities.

The federal government also got involved in recognizing identified gifted students who also had been diagnosed with a disability. Two Board of Cooperative Educational Services (BOCES) districts in Westchester County, New York, established programs as part of federal grants to provide education to gifted students with a handicap. One program began as a full-time elementary class, which eventually grew into a middle and high school gifted special education program. The other program provided strength-based mentorships (Baldwin, Baum, Pereles, & Hughes, 2015). Both programs were very successful and provided models to be duplicated in other school districts such as Montgomery County and Prince George's County, Maryland, and Albuquerque, New Mexico.

1990S DECADE

American legislation in both the field of special education and gifted and talented was in full force during this decade. In 1987 and again in 2001,

Congress authorized a federal project called the Jacob K. Javits Gifted and Talented Students Education Act. It established a National Research Center on the Gifted and Talented (NRC/GT) as well as funded several important three-year demonstration projects placing an educational emphasis on youngsters who were economically disadvantaged and had disabilities who were also gifted (Baum, Shader, & Owen, 2017). The creation of the NRC/GT and completion of the Javits-funded projects both took place during the 1990s.

Similarly, Section 504 of the Rehabilitation Act of 1973 and the Americans with Disabilities Act (ADA), both major legislative acts designed to protect the civil rights of individuals with disabilities, were authorized by Congress in 1990. In addition, a reauthorization of PL 94–142 in 1990 received a new name. PL 94–142 was now known as the Individuals with Disabilities Act (IDEA, 1990; Lerner & Kline, 2006). Finally, the U.S. Department of Education report *National Excellence: A Case for Developing America's Talent* (1993) brought even greater attention to the fact that America was not adequately addressing the needs of its gifted and talented students. In all, these legislative acts paved a more prominent path for special education and gifted and talented services and programs.

SPECIAL EDUCATION PRACTICES

In 1990 Congress authorized Section 504 of the Rehabilitation Act of 1973 and the Americans with Disabilities Act (ADA). Both these major legislative acts were designed to protect the civil rights of individuals with disabilities. Section 504 affords federal funds to be used for supporting special education services in entities such as public schools. ADA funding supports all other entities except for churches and private clubs (Smith, 2001). Both acts broadly define the term "disability" to include "individuals who have a physical or mental impairment that substantially limits one or more of the person's major life activities, has a record of such an impairment, or is regarded as having such an impairment" (Smith, 200, para. 17). Further, students with disabilities are protected from discrimination and are to receive a free, appropriate public education (FAPE) and be allowed to participate in all activities available to students without disabilities such as extracurricular, athletic, and recreational activities and student employment. For students with disabilities, the use of Section 504 and ADA has allowed them to receive the help that they need to participate fully in school.

During a 14-year period beginning in 1990, the Education for All Handicapped Children Act of 1975 (also known as PL 94–142) was reauthorized three times, each time providing more guidelines to assure that the rights and needs of special education students were being met. The first reauthorization became known as the Individuals with Disabilities Act (IDEA; Lerner & Kline, 2006). The reauthorization of IDEA in 1990 added two more disability categories, traumatic brain injury and autism, and required that an individual transition plan be developed to help students transition to postsecondary life. This transition plan included work opportunities as well as further education in the trades or at the college level. Barriers were being broken. This legislation was sending a message and an expectation that individuals with disabilities could lead productive adult lives with meaningful job opportunities commensurate with their abilities.

The reauthorization of IDEA in 1997 emphasized that students with disabilities should have access to the general school curriculum. This resulted in more students being educated in general education classrooms through a process referred to as "mainstreaming" rather than in exclusively segregated special education classrooms or schools. IDEA-1997 also established a mediation process for parents and school districts to resolve educational disputes regarding students' disability services, if any ("A History of the Individuals with Disabilities Education Act," 2023).

GIFTED AND TALENTED PRACTICES

Between 1990 and 2013, the NRC/GT had educational teams who conducted research with the purpose of defining giftedness, identifying programs and services that would benefit gifted students, and evaluating these practices to determine whether they provided positive results for identified students ("The National Research Center on the Gifted and Talented (1990–2013"), n.d.). The NRC/GT research was funded by the federal Javits Act.

Joseph Renzulli, founding director of the NRC/GT, took the previous pedagogy of gifted education and applied it to a school model. This schoolwide enrichment program model (SEM; "Renzulli Center for Creativity, Gifted Education, and Talent Development," n.d.) was not only for gifted students but for all students in the school environment. The purpose of SEM is to provide "enriched learning experiences and higher learning standards for all children through three goals:

- developing talents in all children,
- providing a broad range of advanced-level enrichment experiences for all students, and
- providing advanced follow-up opportunities for young people based on their strengths and interests." (n.d., para. 3)

SEM uses three types of enrichment opportunities for students as identified by Renzulli. The three types of enrichment include:

- all students in a classroom being exposed to a variety of disciplines and enrichment activities (Type I),
- materials and methods used with students that incorporate problem-solving strategies, critical-thinking opportunities, and using affective processes within student specific areas of interest (Type II), and
- students who are interested in more advanced content and who are willing to assume the role of a firsthand inquirer or researcher while participating (Type III; Renzulli & Reis, 2010).

Renzulli (1995) notes, "The SEM approach reflects a democratic ideal that accommodates the full range of individual differences in the entire student population, and it opens the door to programming models that develop the talent potentials of many at-risk students—those often excluded from anything but the most basic of curricular experiences" (p. x).

Two Javits grants, Project High Hopes and the Twice-Exceptional Child Project, made significant inroads to the understanding of gifted students with disabilities. Project High Hopes (Area Cooperative Educational Services [ACES]) located in New Haven, Connecticut, and Cranston, Rhode Island, was a unique program for 130 special education middle-school students who were also gifted. This program gave students the opportunity to engage in activities with authentic content, problem-solving opportunities, and advanced-level thinking activities in their area of strength. During the second year of the three-year research study, some students from Project High Hopes participated in a real-life problem-solving challenge of reconstructing a pond on the campus of the School for the Deaf. To complete the project, these students focused on four domains of study: engineering, performing arts, science, and visual arts. It was quite successful. In the end, the Javits study indicated a student in need of special education services can perform at a level commensurate with their gifted peers without a disability when focusing on a personal strength and/or talent (Baum, Schader, & Owen, 2017).

The Twice-Exceptional Child Project was a collaboration between the Albuquerque, New Mexico, Public School District and the University of New Mexico. The pilot program began in the elementary and middle schools but soon added a high-school component. The researchers studied screening and identification procedures, curriculum, and technology interventions for students who were both identified as gifted and having mild to moderate disabilities. Results led toward a change in terminology for the fields of gifted and special education. The term gifted handicapped and/or gifted learning disabled became twice-exceptional or 2e, terms still used today. Much of the work gathered from the Twice-Exceptional Child Project was used to train teachers in New Mexico as well as across the country (Nielsen, Higgins, Hammond, & Williams, 1993).

Although the Javits grants brought knowledge and attention to the field of gifted students with disabilities, the *National Excellence: A Case for Developing America's Talent* report posited "America demands less of top students than other countries do. At the same time our need for the highest levels of skills and expertise is on the rise, many of America's most talented students are being denied a challenging education" (Office of Educational Research and Improvement, 1993). The report noted that gifted students weren't being academically challenged and that they performed more poorly than gifted students in other countries. Further, most teachers made no provisions academically for gifted students even though many of the identified gifted students knew as much as 50% of the curriculum at the beginning of the school year. The report recommended that communities and schools provide for their gifted students, including those students also identified as disadvantaged and of diverse backgrounds, by offering opportunities to learn advanced materials, receive higher-level learning experiences, and be taught at an academically flexible pace.

2000–2020 DECADES

Beginning in the year 2000, much of the educational legislation went through a reauthorization process. In addition, the fields of special education and gifted and talented education merged more than ever. This created a push toward additional 2e legislation and information dissemination to help all students in an increasingly diverse education system. For example, Congress reauthorized IDEA in 2004, making some serious changes in identification and services for special education students as well as, for the first time, acknowledging that students with disabilities may also have gifts and talents. This was a major step forward for identified twice-exceptional (2e) students.

Further, due to the numerous concerns of policy makers, educators, and parents, the NCLB Act was improved and reauthorized in 2015 as the Every Student Succeeds Act (ESSA). Like any reauthorization, ESSA was an attempt to correct some of the issues in NCLB and previous educational legislation including creating new priorities that all students would have high academic standards to prepare them for college and careers and accountability to effect positive academic change in the lowest-performing schools. Unlike previous legislation, ESSA would finally increase academic expectations and standards to include gifted students while, at the same time, benefiting students who were identified as academically at-risk and/or struggling.

SPECIAL EDUCATION PRACTICES

The reauthorization of IDEA in 2004 changed the way school districts identified students with learning disabilities. Previously, special educators used the discrepancy model in which students needed to demonstrate a significant delay between an expected versus actual level of achievement in reading and math to be considered in need of disability services. Educators frequently referred to this discrepancy model as the "wait to fail" model because so many students with learning disabilities were failing when they were finally identified and began receiving services. IDEA 2004 required districts to provide early intervention services for children not identified for special education services but who needed additional academic and behavioral support to succeed in general education classes. This new, more proactive process was known as response to intervention (RtI). RtI required educators to use research-based techniques and materials to identify and teach their at-risk students.

While RtI focused on students who were at-risk for academic failure, many schools moved to the more comprehensive multitiered systems of support (MTSS) model. MTSS uses academic information as well as behavioral, social, and emotional issues that affect the whole child when identifying students in need of services. The key components of both RtI and MTSS are:

- a tiered system of support and interventions,
- early intervention prior to formal identification,
- screening, assessments, and progress monitoring,
- standard protocol interventions, and
- collaborative problem solving and planning for the child with the parents (Coleman & Hughes, 2009).

Although most educators think of RtI and MTSS as a special education initiative, many educators and researchers state that both can be used effectively with identified gifted and talented and twice-exceptional students (Hughes & Dexter, 2011; Hughes et al., 2011).

GIFTED AND TALENTED SERVICES

In 2002, ESEA was reauthorized by Congress as the No Child Left Behind Act (NCLB). The goal of NCLB was to improve education for all students. States were required to establish achievement standards and yearly assessment tools to measure students' academic progress in basic skills. School report cards were shared with parents and communities to indicate how both individual students and the school's student body were doing on these standardized assessments. Because teacher ratings were based on these report cards and standardized test scores, it was frequently reported that teachers were focusing most of their time and energy on helping at-risk and average-level students pass the tests. This educational practice meant that many gifted and high achieving students were being ignored because it was thought that this group of students would "pass" the standardized assessments without any issue. This fallacy hurt many gifted students who did not receive an education commensurate with their higher-level thinking and cognitive abilities.

In 2004, an important book in the field of gifted education, *A Nation Deceived: How Schools Hold Back America's Brightest Students* (Colangelo, Assouline, & Gross) was published. This monumental document focused on academic acceleration, stating that even with 50 years of research indicating acceleration was positive, productive, and necessary for identified gifted students, acceleration as a concept was misunderstood and rarely used. Eighteen forms of acceleration were listed, and the document discussed why it was important to align the form of acceleration with the readiness and needs of the individual student. *A Nation Deceived* also acknowledged that most educators continued to resist the research-based information and the "educational establishment, especially at the elementary and middle school levels, remains skeptical based on implications of ruined scope and sequence charts and ungrounded fears of hampering healthy social-emotional adjustment" (Colangelo et al., 2004, p. ix).

Further research and activity on twice-exceptional students included continued support for the Jacob Javits federal grants and Project2Excel. The Javits grants continued to focus on underrepresented, economically disadvantaged, limited English proficient (LEP), and students with disabilities in gifted and talented programs and ways to reduce the serious gap in achievement among certain student groups that should be at the highest levels of achievement. The Minnesota Project2Excel conducted a five-year study beginning in 2008 of gifted elementary and middle-school students who had various exceptionalities, including those students identified with attention deficit disorders, autism spectrum disorders, behavioral and emotional disorders, and learning disabilities. Project2Excel sought to train classroom teachers and provide them with a toolkit of gifted curriculum accommodations to use with 2e students. This group also created resource manuals, ongoing professional development sessions for teachers and parents, and a twice-exceptional certification course (*About the Project*, 2023).

Simultaneously, states such as Maryland, Idaho, Ohio, and Virginia were taking the initiative to address the needs of their twice-exceptional learners by publishing policy guides or by providing services, grants, and staff development for teachers and school districts. Further, the Colorado Department of Education provided grants to give school districts the opportunity to identify and serve their 2e students while training their teachers. Their Twice-Exceptional Project team developed manuals, training modules, and resources that educators and parents from all over the state could access.

With new 2e research, many articles, books,[3] newsletters,[4] and other publications began to appear in major professional journals and be distributed to describe characteristics and needs of the 2e population. Valuable and varied resources for both parents and educators continued to become more common as did advocacy organizations such as Twice Exceptional Children's Advocacy (TECA), the National Association of Gifted Children (NAGC) 2e Special Interest Group, Bright and Quirky, and With Understanding Comes Calm. Further, Bridges Graduate School of Cognitive Diversity in Education was established in 2005 and began offering doctoral and master's degrees as well as certification in the field of twice exceptionality.

Although labeling a child as learning disabled, ADHD, and/or in need of services for autism spectrum disorder was meant to provide them with the services and education they needed, many special education and 2e students often feel stigmatized by these labels. However, a new and unexpected phenomenon began that made being identified as having a disability more palatable. More and more successful entrepreneurs and business CEOs began publicly revealing their personal struggles and disabilities. From Malcolm Gladwell's book (2015), *David and Goliath: Underdogs, Misfits, and the Art of Battling Giants*:

> Richard Branson, the British billionaire entrepreneur, is dyslexic. Charles Schwab, the founder of the discount brokerage that bears his name, is dyslexic, as are the cell phone pioneer Craig McCaw; David Neeleman, the founder of JetBlue; John Chambers, the CEO of the technology giant Cisco; Paul Orfalea, the founder of Kinko's—to name just a few. (p. 106)

There are two interpretations of this information that 2e children can identify with. First, the identified giftedness of these entrepreneurs allowed them to overcome their disabilities. Second, these individuals succeeded because their disability taught them to be resilient and to "think outside the box" when successfully creating new or improved services.

In 2014, stakeholders from various organizations and educational fields came together to form the first National 2e Community of Practice (2eCoP) intent on finding common ground to develop a unified definition for twice-exceptionality. This definition "would allow the [2e] field to move toward a more cohesive, meaningful understanding of twice exceptionality and the needed, appropriate supports" (Baldwin et al., 2015, p. 212).

The 26 members of 2eCoP represented national, state, and local organizations such as the National Association for Gifted Children (NAGC), the Council for Exceptional Children (CEC), the National Center for Learning Disabilities (NCLD), the University of Iowa Belin-Blank Center for Gifted Education, Johns Hopkins University, and the University of Connecticut. Using a consensus approach, the following agreed-upon definition prevailed:

> Twice-exceptional (2e) individuals evidence exceptional ability and disability, which results in a unique set of circumstances. Their exceptional ability may dominate, hiding their disability; their disability may dominate, hiding their exceptional ability; each may mask the other so that neither is recognized or addressed.
>
> 2e students, who may perform below, at, or above grade level, require the following:
>
> - Specialized methods of identification that consider the possible interaction of the exceptionalities,
> - Enriched/advanced education opportunities that develop the child's interests, gifts, and talents while also meeting the child's learning needs, and
> - Simultaneous supports that ensure the child's academic success and social-emotional well-being, such as accommodations, therapeutic interventions, and specialized instruction.
>
> Working successfully with this unique population requires specialized academic training and ongoing professional development. (CEC-TAG, 2022)

The "masking issue" discussed in the 2e definition has made identifying twice-exceptional students difficult in the general education classroom (Baldwin, Omdal, & Pereles, 2015; Baum et al., 2017; Omdal, 2015). Part of the problem is a lack of training for educators. Although there has been a plethora of research, articles, books, and internet sites on twice-exceptionality topics, the general education teacher rarely receives training on how to identify these special students or if identified, how to meet their individual educational needs.

Another aspect of the 2e definition that resonates with many educators and parents is the need to provide the student with both opportunities to develop and express their gifts and talents while receiving accommodations, modifications, and special services necessary allowing the student to show success. Numerous educators and researchers in the 2e field (Baldwin et al., 2015; Baum et al., 2017; Kircher-Morris, 2021) highly recommend a strength-based, talent-focused education be provided for students with twice-exceptionalities. As noted by Baum, Schader, and Owen (2017),

The belief that 2e students' deficits must be remediated before attention can be given to their abilities and interest often results in little or inappropriate attention to students' gifts or talents. Moreover, because the remediation techniques usually lack the characteristics high-ability students require for successful learning, many remedial attempts are unsuccessful. (p. 53)

Some students remain underserved and struggle with the reality of inequitable access to resources and services in U.S. public schools. Four groups of students are identified as underserved gifted learners. According to Ritchotte et al. (2020), these groups include students with culturally and linguistically diverse (CLD) backgrounds, English language learners (ELLs), economically disadvantaged students, and students identified as twice-exceptional (2e). Davis and Robinson (2004) agree, "The underrepresentation of culturally diverse gifted students is a pervasive and egregious problem across the nation . . . Although Black and Latino students combined make up 42% of the student populations in schools that have gifted and advanced learner programs nationwide, they comprise only 28% of the students identified and enrolled in those programs" (p. 278).

As the number of ELLs in U.S. public schools continues to increase (Richotte et al., 2020), it is important not to lose those diverse students who have potential for gifted performance. Identifying ELLs for gifted programs is difficult because so many identification procedures are verbally oriented and stress academic accomplishment as a primary decision point for qualification into a gifted program. Frequently, ELL students who have learned to communicate effectively in English in a social setting still have challenges with the complexity of academic English. Having continued difficulty with academic English, often seen on standardized assessments, makes it difficult for these students to perform at a proficient level. In addition, Gentry and Seward (2018) note that, "Gifted students from low-income families may be the most invisible group in education today" (p. 354). This is due to typically low expectations, teacher bias, and a focus on deficits and disadvantages of these students rather than on higher level thinking and creativity. A gifted student from disadvantaged circumstances who does not receive the academic challenges in elementary school, thus allowing him to demonstrate his capabilities, may lag behind academically by high school, resulting in the prospect of higher level, advanced courses or even college becoming impossible.

CONCLUSION

The 60-year review of two specific fields of education, special education and the education of the gifted and talented, results in a mixed outcome. In the

1960s, few services were available for individuals with disabilities and those that did exist were inadequate, stigmatizing, and demeaning. Students identified in need of special education services frequently ended up in segregated classes away from their peers or worse yet, were sent to institutions. By 2020, significant improvements had been made in the way we, as a society, treat and educate individuals with disabilities. In large part due to federal legislation and funding, students with disabilities are now primarily educated in inclusive settings and receive individualized services, through an IEP or 504 plan, both tailored to meet the student's educational and social/emotional needs. Although we've progressed as a society and in the field of education, we still do not totally accept and understand diverse or different individuals for their unique learning and social/emotional needs. As we move forward, neurocognitive research will help the field of special education by focusing its attention on how the brain learns and processes information even with a disability present. At the same time, researchers, educators, and parents need to continue advocating for the field of special education to focus on and teach toward students' strengths and talents rather than focusing on what they cannot do.

A similar positive progression may not exist in the field of gifted and talented education. Unlike special education, where the trajectory has been positive and growth oriented over the past 60 years, gifted education continues to resemble a roller-coaster ride. In some years, educating the brightest students has been valued. Many other years, funds were abolished, causing many schools to eliminate their gifted programs altogether. The U.S. government has not provided a consistent vision, legislation, or funding for gifted education and its services during the past six decades.

Similarly, many states have not done much better providing leadership or policies to educate their students identified as needing gifted and talented programming and services. Surveys and data on gifted and talented students, programs, and services conducted by NAGC and the Council of State Directors of Programs for the Gifted (CSDPG; Rinn, Mun, & Hodges, 2020) report that only fifteen states provide both a mandate and funding for identification, programming, and services for identified gifted and talented students. As of 2020, New York City, one of the biggest school districts in the country, was still undecided about whether to eliminate its district-wide gifted and talented programs.

Without consistent federal funding and policies, students who have the potential for the highest levels of achievement and creativity are left to the whims and budgets of individual school districts and state-wide policies. These uncertainties will continue to make it difficult to educate and meet the academic, social, and emotional needs of gifted students—including those from diverse and underserved populations. The risk is too great for the field of gifted and talented education to not advocate the importance of properly educating and supporting all the needs of these cognitively able students.

The field of twice-exceptional education (2e) bridges both special education and gifted education. The field of 2e has seen significant changes and growth since its inception in the 1980s when students were referred to as "gifted underachievers" or "gifted handicapped." There was little known about this population of students. Due to federal and state grants fiscally supporting research, directed staff development opportunities, and an investment in student learning programs and strategies, a greater interest and understanding of this special population of students remains. However, identifying and providing appropriate services for 2e students remains elusive. Except for some regions of the United States, most of the information surrounding twice-exceptionality has not penetrated the general education arena. Those 2e students rarely are identified or receive individualized services in many public-school settings. The issues of early 2e identification, teacher training, and strength-based, talent-focused programming needs to continue to be the focus as the field of twice-exceptionality moves into the future.

Sixty years ago, President Kennedy challenged American citizens to get involved, to make a difference, and to be part of a solution. Although many educators took up this challenge and have made a difference in the field of education, more work needs to be done to ensure that every student can demonstrate her innate potential. We need to value and respect all students for their strengths and their challenges, finding ways to celebrate their uniqueness.

NOTES

1. The other organizations included in this meeting to make up the National Joint Committee for Learning Disabilities (NJCLD) were: the American Speech-Language-Hearing Association (ASHA), the Association for Children and Adults with Learning Disabilities (ACLD), the Council for Learning Disabilities (CLD), the Division for Children with Communication Disorders (DCCD), the International Reading Association (IRA), and the Orton Dyslexia Society (formerly the Orton Society) (Hammill, Leigh, McNutt, and Larsen, 1981).

2. The updated version of Gardner's Theory of Multiple Intelligences (MI) includes *eight* categories: spatial, bodily-kinesthetic, musical, linguistic, logical-mathematical, interpersonal, intrapersonal, and naturalistic/nature intelligence (Gardner, 201).

3. Books on 2e student populations include *Learning outside the Lines: Two Ivy League Students with Learning Disabilities and ADHD Give You the Tools for Academic Success and Educational Revolution* (Mooney & Cole, 2000); *Twice-Exceptional and Special Populations of Gifted Students (Essential Readings in Gifted Education Series)*, 1st ed. (Baum & Reis, 2004); *Smart Kids with*

Learning Difficulties: Overcoming Obstacles and Realizing Potential, 2nd ed. (Weinfeld, Barnes-Robinson, Jeweler, & Shevitz, 2013); *To Be Gifted and Learning Disabled: Strength Based Strategies for Helping Twice-Exceptional Students with LD, ADHD, SD, and More*, 3rd ed. (Baum, Schader, & Owen, 2017); *Twice-Exceptional: Supporting and Educating Bright and Creative Students with Learning Difficulties*, 1st ed. (Kaufman, 2018); *Seeing and Serving Underserved Gifted Students: 50 Strategies for Equity and Excellence* (Ritchotte, Lee, & Graefe, 2019).

4. Examples of electronic newsletters/resources include 2e Newsletter, https://www.2enews.com/; and Smart Kids with Learning Disabilities https://www.smartkidswithld.org/.

REFERENCES

About the project. (2023). University of St. Thomas Project2Excel. Retrieved January 18, 2023, https://www.stthomas.edu/project2excel/about-the-project/

American Speech-Language-Hearing Association. (1997, February 1). *Operationalizing the NJCLD definition of learning disabilities for ongoing assessment in schools.* https://www.asha.org/policy/rp1998-00130/#:~:text=Learning%20disabilities%20is%20a%20general,%2C%20reasoning%2C%20or%20mathematical%20skills

Baldwin, L., Baum, S., Pereles, D., & Hughes, C. (2015). Twice-exceptional learners: The journey toward a shared vision. *Gifted Child Today, 38*(4), 206–214. https://losangeles.bridges.edu/uploads/6/3/7/5/63751333/gct_article--_history_of_the_field.pdf

Baldwin, L., Omdal, S., & Pereles, D. (2015). Beyond stereotypes: Understanding, recognizing, and working with twice-exceptional learners. *Teaching Exceptional Children, 47*(4), 216–225.

Bard, B., & Fletcher, J. (1968). The right to die. *Atlantic Monthly, 221,* 58–64.

Baum, S. M., & Reis, S. M. (Eds.). (2004). *Twice-exceptional and special populations of gifted students (Essential readings in gifted education series),* 1st ed. Corwin.

Baum, S. M., Shader, R. M., & Owen, S. V. (2017). *To be gifted and learning disabled: Strength-based strategies for helping twice-exceptional students with LD, ADHD, ASD, and more,* 3rd ed. Routledge.

CEC-TAG. (2022). *2e definition.* CEC-TAG. https://cectag.com/about-tag/2e-definition

Colangelo, N., Assouline, S. G., & Gross, M. U. M. (2004). *A nation deceived: How schools hold back America's brightest students.* Connie Belin & Jacqueline N. Blank International Center for Gifted Education and Talent Development, University of Iowa.

Coleman, M. R., & Hughes, C. E. (2009). Meeting the needs of gifted students within an RtI framework. *Gifted Child Today Magazine, 32*(3), 14–17. https://doi.org/10.1177/107621750903200306

Davis, J. L., & Robinson, S. A. (2018). Being 3e, a new look at culturally diverse gifted learners with exceptional conditions: An examination of the issues and solutions for educators and families. *Twice exceptional: Supporting and educating bright and creative students with learning difficulties, 18*, 278–289.

Education for All Handicapped Children Act (EHA; also known as PL 94–142). (1975). https://www.govinfo.gov/content/pkg/STATUTE-89/pdf/STATUTE-89-Pg773.pdf#page=1

Fisher, J. (Director). (1996). *Unforgotten: Twenty-five years after willowbrook.* City Lights International.

Fox, L., Brody, L., & Tobin, D. (Eds). (1983). *Learning-disabled/gifted children: Identification and programming.* University Park Press.

Gamson, D. A., McDermott, K.A., & Reed, D. S. (2015, December). The elementary and secondary education act at fifty: Aspirations, effects, and limitations. *Russell Sage Foundation Journal of the Social Sciences, 1*(3), 1–29. https://doi.org/10.7758/RSF.2015.1.3.01

Gardner, H. E. (2011). *Frames of mind: The theory of multiple intelligences.* Basic Books.

Gentry, M., & Seward, K. (2018). Gifted students from low-socioeconomic backgrounds. In J. L. Roberts, T. F. Inman, & J. H. Robins (Eds.), *Introduction to gifted education* (pp. 353–368). Prufrock.

Gifted and Talented Children's Education Act, Public Law 95–561. (1978). https://www.govinfo.gov/content/pkg/STATUTE-92/pdf/STATUTE-92-Pg2143.pdf

Gladwell, M. (2015). *David and Goliath: Underdogs, misfits, and the art of battling giants.* Back Bay Books.

Goddard, H. H. (1920). *Human efficiency and levels of intelligence.* Princeton University Press.

Hammill, D. D., Leigh, J. E., McNutt, G., & Larsen, S. C. (1988). A new definition of learning disabilities. *Learning Disability Quarterly, 11*(3), 217–223.

Hughes, C. & Dexter, D. D. (2011). Response to intervention: A research-based summary. *Theory into Practice, 50*(1), 4–11. https://doi.org/10.1080/00405841.2011.534909

Hughes, C., Rollins, K., Johnsen, S. K., Pereles, D., Omdal, S., Baldwin, L., Brown, E., Abernethy, S., & Coleman, M. R. (2011). Challenges for including gifted education within an RtI model. In Mary Ruth Coleman & Susan K. Johnsen (Eds.), *RtI for gifted students: A CEC-TAG educational resource* (pp. 119–27). Prufrock Press.

Jacob K. Javits Gifted and Talented Students Education Act of 2001. Pub. L. 89–10, title V, §5461, as added Pub. L. 107–110, title V, §501, Jan. 8, 2002, 115 Stat. 1826.

John F. Kennedy Presidential Library and Museum. (n.d.). *John F. Kennedy and people with intellectual disabilities.* jfklibrary.org. https://www.jfklibrary.org/learn/about-jfk/jfk-in-history/john-f-kennedy-and-people-with-intellectual-disabilities

Jolly, J. L., & Robins, J. H. (2022). History of gifted education. In J. L. Roberts, T. F. Inman, & J. L. Jolly (Eds.), *Introduction to gifted education* (pp. 19–34). Prufrock.

Kaufman, S. B. (Ed.). (2018). *Twice-exceptional: Supporting and educating bright and creative students with learning difficulties.* Oxford University Press.

Kingsley, J., & Levitz, M. (2007). *Count us in: Growing up with Down Syndrome.* Harcourt.

Kircher-Morris, E. (2021). *Teaching twice-exceptional learners in today's classroom*. Free Spirit Publishing.

Lerner, J. W., & Kline, F. (2006). *Learning disabilities and related disorders: Characteristics and teaching strategies* (10th ed.). Houghton Mifflin.

Maker, C. J. (1977). *Providing programs for the gifted handicapped*. Council for Exceptional Children (CEC).

Marland, Jr., S. P. (1971). *The Marland report*. Department of Health, Education, and Welfare: Office of Education. https://files.eric.ed.gov/fulltext/ED056243.pdf

Meldon, P. (2017, October 31). *Disability history: Early and shifting attitudes of treatment*. National Park Service. https://www.nps.gov/articles/disabilityhistoryearlytreatment.htm

Mooney, J., & Cole, D. (2000). *Learning outside the lines: Two Ivy League students with learning disabilities and ADHD give you the tools for academic success and educational revolution*. Touchstone.

NAEG School of Education. (n.d.). *Renzulli Center for Creativity, Gifted Education, and Talent Development*. gifted.uconn.edu, https://gifted.uconn.edu/schoolwide-enrichment-model/

National Education Association. (2020). *History of standardized testing in the United States*. https://www.nea.org/professional-excellence/student-engagement/tools-tips/history-standardized-testing-united-states

Newnham, N., & LeBrecht, J. (Directors). (2020). *Crip camp* [Film]. Higher Ground Productions, Little Punk, Ford Foundation, Just Films, Rusted Spoke Productions.

Nielsen, M. E., Higgins, L. D., Hammond, A. E., & Williams, R. A. (1993). Gifted children with disabilities. *Gifted Child Today, 16*(5), 9–12.

Office of Educational Research and Improvement (1993). *National excellence: A case for developing America's talent*. Office of Educational Research and Improvement. https://files.eric.ed.gov/fulltext/ED359743.pdf

Omdal, S. (2015). Twice exceptionality from a practitioner's perspective. *Gifted Child Today Magazine, 38*(4), 246–248. https://doi.org/10.1177/1076217515597287

Renzulli Center for Creativity, Gifted Education, and Talent Development. (n.d.) *The National Research Center on the Gifted and Talented (1990–2013)*. nrcgt.uconn.edu, https://nrcgt.uconn.edu/

Renzulli, J. S. (1995). *Building a bridge between gifted education and total school improvement*. National Research Center on the Gifted and Talented (NRC/GT). https://files.eric.ed.gov/fulltext/ED388013.pdf

Renzulli, J. S. (1978). What makes giftedness? Re-examining a definition. *Phi Delta Kappan, 60*, 180–184, 261.

Renzulli, J. S. (2022). *The Three Ring Conception of Giftedness*. renzullilearning.com. https://renzullilearning.com/en/Menus/7-researchbased-learning-system#:~:text=The%20Three%20Ring%20Conception%20of%20Giftedness&text=The%20Three%20Rings%20include%3A%20Above,three%20traits%20exhibit%20gifted%20behavior

Renzulli, J. S., & Reis, S. M. (2010). The Schoolwide Enrichment Model: A focus on student strengths and interests. *Gifted Education International, 26*(2–3), 140–156. https://doi.org/10.1177/026142941002600303

Rinn, A. N., Mun, R. U., & Hodges, J. (2020). 2018–2019 State of the States in Gifted Education. National Association for Gifted Children and the Council of State Directors of Programs for the Gifted. https://www.nagc.org/2018-2019-state-states-gifted-education

Ritchotte, J., Lee, C-W, & Graefe, A. (2019). *Seeing and serving underserved gifted students: 50 strategies for equity and excellence.* Free Spirit Publishing.

Shriver, E. K. (1962). Hope for retarded children. *Saturday Evening Post*, 252, 71–75. https://www.saturdayeveningpost.com/wp-content/uploads/satevepost/1962-eunice-kennedy.pdf

Smith, T. E. C. (2001). Section 504, the ADA, and Public Schools. *Remedial and Special Education, 22*(6), 335–343.

Solomon, A. (2012). *Far from the tree: Parents, children, and the search for identity.* Scribner.

Special Olympics. (2022). *History.* specialolympics.org, https://www.specialolympics.org/about/history/1968-games?locale=en

Strauss, V. (2013, October 16). Howard Gardner: "Multiple intelligences" are not "learning styles." *Washington Post.* https://www.washingtonpost.com/news/answer-sheet/wp/2013/10/16/howard-gardner-multiple-intelligences-are-not-learning-styles/

Tannenbaum, A. J. (1983). *Gifted children: Psychological and educational perspectives.* Macmillan.

The Patient Protection and Affordable Care Act, Publ. L. No. 111–148, 124 Stat. 119 (2010). https://www.govinfo.gov/content/pkg/PLAW-111publ148/pdf/PLAW-111publ148.pdf

United States Department of Education Individuals with Disabilities Education Act. (2022). *A History of the Individuals with Disabilities Education Act.* https://sites.ed.gov/idea/IDEA-History

United States Senate. (n.d.). *Sputnik spurs passage of the National Defense Education Act.* senate.gov. https://www.senate.gov/artandhistory/history/minute/Sputnik_Spurs_Passage_of_National_Defense_Education_Act.htm#:~:text=The%20National%20Defense%20Education%20Act%20of%201958%20became%20one%20of,and%20private%20colleges%20and%20universities

Weinfeld, R., Barnes-Robinson, L., Jeweler, S., & Shevitz, B. R. (2013). *Smart kids with learning difficulties: Overcoming obstacles and realizing potential,* 2nd ed. Routledge.

Chapter 4

An Evolving Understanding of the Autism Spectrum

A Practitioner's Journey

Joanne McMahon

In the 1990s, research on the autism spectrum was reaching a fever pitch, and national conferences on the topic abounded. Over the years, with increased understanding of children with disabilities, families began to seek placement options in their local school districts and away from center-based settings. Parents wanted more normalized education opportunities in accordance with the law's (PL 94–142) mandate of students identified with disabilities having the option of a less restrictive environment. School districts, private schools, and agencies sought professional development and counsel for general and special education teachers, administrators, and paraprofessional staff. They needed to prepare for the influx of children identified on the autism spectrum entering public school environments.

Very early on, one of the many obstacles to be overcome in the field of special education and the education hierarchy was the stigma society placed on children with disabilities. Most conditions affecting social, cognitive, behavior, learning, and motor development were little or poorly understood. This lack of understanding was especially attached to children diagnosed with autism (Colker, 2013). Blame and shame were rampant, placed especially on mothers of children with autism.

The Kennedy family exerted tremendous influence on society and public policy related to children identified with disabilities in the 1960s and beyond. Although President Kennedy's tenure was cut short by his tragic assassination, his administration had started to shape policy as it related to people identified as disabled. Kennedy's presidency also introduced us to his extended family, particularly to his sister Eunice Kennedy Shriver, who exhibited courage and forthrightness in divulging to the world the existence of their long-hidden sister, Rosemary. Unlike her personable, athletic, and high-achieving siblings, Rosemary suffered from intellectual deficits and maladaptive behavior and had been placed out of society for many decades, a common practice at the time. Eunice Kennedy Shriver lifted the veil of humiliation and ignominy suffered by families with an atypical member and paved the way for others with disabilities to live in society.

Eunice Kennedy Shriver, motivated to advocate for individuals with disabilities, founded the Special Olympics. Today, it is the largest worldwide sports organization for children and adults identified with intellectual and/or physical disabilities. The advocacy work of such a prominent person as Eunice initiated a sea change, paving the way for ongoing advances on behalf of children and adults identified with disabilities. In addition, the Eunice Kennedy Shriver Center at the University of Massachusetts Medical School conducts research and provides support and educational programs to individuals identified with intellectual disabilities. Presently, Robert F. Kennedy Jr., son of U.S. Senator Robert F. Kennedy and nephew of President John F. Kennedy, continues the family's advocacy through the establishment of the Children's Health Defense Organization. Its goal is to raise awareness of the negative effects of environmental factors and health care policy on the overall health of all people, with particular attention paid to individuals identified with autism spectrum disorders.

Early in my teaching career, I developed empathy and deep respect for the families and especially the parents of my special education students. I also experienced a disparity between the minimal regulations granted by PL 94–142 and what was necessary for these children to thrive in the school classroom. If specific strategies, techniques, and practices were not applied, these children would not receive an optimal level of academic instruction and would fail to learn fundamental life skills for future success. In the absence of proper training for new and experienced teachers and clinicians, there would be little to no difference between the practice of special education and general education.

In early clinical and higher education circles, many educators believed that autism was caused by a "refrigerator mother." Who and what exactly was a refrigerator mother? The 1970s theory posited that such a mother was emotionally aloof and detached from her child, sometimes even neglectful, thus causing the child to withdraw from the world (Cohmer, 2014). Refrigerator mother was a label for mothers of children diagnosed with autism or schizophrenia. Parents, particularly mothers, were often blamed for their children's atypical behavior, which included rigid rituals, speech difficulty, and self-isolation.

In some parts of the world, the refrigerator mother theory remained in practice for many decades. For novices entering the field of special education today, this prominent theory seems absurd for a condition now understood to be a neurodevelopmental disorder. However, back in the 1970s, much of psychiatry was based on a nature versus nurture debate with nurture assuming the dominant role in etiology. Today's more current and updated terminology references ASD as having a basis in genetics versus environmental factors, thus replacing the nature/nurture origin.

Even with some skepticism, the refrigerator mother theory remained a part of many traditional graduate school program vernacular. As a fifth-year teacher, I met my first student who carried a diagnosis of this rare disorder. He was a handsome child with a John John Kennedy hairstyle and beautiful blue eyes. His preferred way to communicate was to approach peers and staff with a broad and beautiful smile and yell out, "Clum, Clum!" His young mother arrived one afternoon for a parent-teacher conference. Speaking with that sweet, loving, attentive woman, I recall thinking, *There is NO way this mother caused this child to develop the way he did.* There was more to learn about this diagnosis, and I was eager to help push the fields of psychology and education toward a more accurate diagnosis and overall understanding of these fascinating children.

WHAT IS AUTISM SPECTRUM DISORDER?

Considered the quintessential disability enigma, autism spectrum disorder is a lifelong neurodevelopmental disorder. The puzzle piece logo used by many advocacy groups and conference organizers is meant to indicate that even in the 21st century, all the pieces of this complex condition are not yet fully identified, researched, or understood. Yet, magnificent progress has been made since the early days of the refrigerator mother theory in uncovering this complex disorder.

Autism was once considered a low-incidence disorder, but now it is a common household word. Initially, it was considered a form of childhood schizophrenia. Until the mid-1940s, autism was viewed as the result of poor nurturing by the mother. Leo Kanner (1894–1981), the father of child psychiatry from Johns Hopkins University Hospital, is reportedly the first to use the phrase "early infantile autism" (Kanner, 2019). His initial study on autism was published in 1943 and is considered groundbreaking. Kanner centered his study around children belonging to a distinct clinical group and labeled them as Kanner Syndrome children. Kanner also believed that refrigerator mothers had everything to do with their child being born with autism tendencies. Over the years that followed, Kanner's 1943 study elevated autism to the forefront of child psychiatry. The study paved the way for children to not only be identified properly but laid the foundation for truer diagnoses of individuals with autism. In the 1968 version of the *Diagnostic and Statistical Manual (DSM)-II*, "autistic, atypical, and withdrawn behavior" was still associated with schizophrenia in children. Not until the *DSM-III* in 1980 would infantile autism appear as a diagnosis separate from schizophrenia (American Psychiatric Association, 2014). It took 40 years for the term "autism" to appear in the 1980 edition of the *DSM-III* as a standalone, pervasive developmental disorder. A pervasive developmental disorder is a subgroup of disorders characterized by delays in the development of socialization and communication skills.

In the 1994 edition of the *DSM-IV*, autism was labeled as "autistic disorder" with five subcategories: Asperger's disorder, pervasive developmental disorder, NOS (not otherwise specified), Rett's disorder, and childhood disintegrative disorder. In addition, there were 16 possible diagnostic criteria for any of the subcategories under the "autistic disorder" heading. This differentiation helped in identifying an autistic disorder but left the overall understanding of autism a challenge.

The current edition of the *DSM-V* (2015) combined the five separate disorders under the category of autism spectrum disorder (ASD). The term *spectrum* refers to the broad range of severity, intensity, and variations in the expression of the common traits associated with a disorder. This *DSM-V* revision caused a great deal of controversy in the psychiatry and advocacy communities. Many believed a combination of disorders negated greater precision and understanding of the disability, which could lead to denial of services and opportunities for children and their families.

Currently, spectrum disorders are strongly believed to be genetic brain-based disorders or disruptions resulting from defects in genes that control brain development and regulate how brain cells communicate with each other (Maloney, Rieger, & Dougherty, 2013). Some research of spectrum disorders also points to systemic disorders, or those disorders affecting not just the brain but other bodily tissues as well. The latter theory concludes that systemically the genes passed on from parent to child may exhibit varying degrees of vulnerability to environmental factors such as chemicals and infectious microbes, resulting in possible malfunction and linked to ASD (Maloney, Rieger, & Dougherty, 2013).

The *DSM-V* study group believes the creation of the ASD single category best reflects what is now known about autism, its behaviors, and understandings. More than $1 billion were spent in the past decade trying to identify causes of spectrum disorders such as autism. Despite a plethora of funding and research, myriad data and information have failed to complete the bigger, more absolute picture of this disability.

DEFINING FEATURES OF A SPECTRUM DISORDER

As stated, criteria established for diagnosis of a spectrum disorder in the *DSM-V* have been consolidated. Although primarily understood as an impairment in social interaction, autism spectrum disorders also impact language development and include significant behavioral traits in the form of restricted interests and patterns of behavior. Children and adults diagnosed with autism spectrum disorder exhibit dozens upon dozens of traits and characteristics unique to each individual, leading to the familiar adage, "If you know one child with autism, you know one child with autism."

Blanketing these traits are sensory sensitivities, medical conditions, and associated comorbid features. Medical conditions can include sleep disturbance, gastrointestinal disorders, autoimmune vulnerabilities, allergies, and seizures. Among the many associated features are intellectual disabilities, anxiety, learning disabilities, executive functioning deficits, problems with impulse control, self-injurious behaviors, tantrums, pica, and aggression. Coexisting with the diagnosis of ASD, one can also be diagnosed with anxiety disorder, obsessive compulsive disorder, depression, attention deficit/ hyperactivity disorder, or Tourette syndrome. Nonetheless, a spectrum disorder is marked by significant impairments in four distinct areas of development: lack of social instinct, acquisition and use of language, restrictive and repetitive behavior, and sensory sensitivities. These developmental areas will be described in more detail below.

Lack of Social Instinct

The hallmark of any spectrum disorder is a marked contrast in the social development of the child compared to neurotypical development as seen in other children. Many of these children exhibit neurobiological differences, which appear in varied degrees. Children with spectrum disorders choose and prefer solitary activities such as playing alone with a ball or toy. They often interact with others as if they were objects without feeling or appropriate emotional response and have difficulty imitating others and taking turns.

The development of friendships or most peer relationships fail without targeted teaching of social skills. As a result, social situations and social cues are often misread. There can be sensitivity to criticism or correction, a low response to social praise, and limited use and understanding of personal body language and facial expressions in these situations. There exists an innate lack of awareness of other people's feelings including demonstrating sympathy, empathy, or altruism, and children diagnosed with a spectrum disorder can appear rude or impolite. An inability to engage in social and emotional reciprocity or a disinterest or lack of awareness of what pleases others may exist. Awareness of these and other traits showing diminutive signs of social instinct in children diagnosed with ASD are critical to develop prescriptive strategies that will build social skill sets needed for ongoing social development.

Acquisition and Use of Language

The acquisition and general use of language by children diagnosed with ASD is varied and diverse. In my experience, some children are extremely verbal with sophisticated vocabularies that often seem "scripted" in delivery. According to the *DSM-IV*, others never acquire oral language. Many children diagnosed with ASD fall in the middle, often asking numerous repetitive questions. These children are often delayed talkers if they can communicate orally at all.

Due to their neurodevelopmental differences, children with ASD fail to understand the critical use of language when getting basic needs met, promoting social interactions with others, and finding success in completion of daily living activities. Other examples of language challenges include discrepancies in the development of both receptive and expressive language (impacting the understanding of the spoken word), deficits in vocabulary development, nonuse or lack of understanding of body language, various parts of speech, concept development, pragmatic language (using our voice, language, and bodies to communicate our personal thoughts, ideas, and feelings), and paralinguistics (vocal and nonvocal signals including accent, pitch, volume, speech rate, modulation, and fluency). Some ASD children fail to respond to greetings and slang; often idioms and terms of endearment are misunderstood. For children who never acquire oral language or have limited language use, assistive technology is required. Such technology includes the picture exchange communication system, augmentative communication systems, or basic sign language. In recent times, iPad applications and computers increase the ability for students identified with ASD and needing additional services to communicate well with others around them.

Restrictive and Repetitive Behavior

Individuals identified with a spectrum disorder have a strong desire to maintain sameness and are resistant to changes in their routine or environment. Some types of restrictive behaviors can be seen in the home environment. For example, many families enjoy routines such as Friday night pizza. However, an identified autistic child in this family will require the pizza to be the same variety and from the same exact shop week after week, creating enormous pressure on the family system when restricting the family from enjoying different types of pizza. Parents often have to drive the exact car route each time the family leaves the house or cajole autistic children who resist or refuse to change seasonal clothing when shorts and T-shirts must be replaced by long-sleeve shirts and pants. Differences in eating habits, family routines, or changes in clothing might be detected instantaneously and cause anxiety or confusion for a child with autism. As a result, families can get locked into these patterns of sameness and rituals but may benefit from learning various techniques to help create flexibility in their child.

I have observed that children identified with a spectrum disorder may exhibit another repetitive behavior, manifested as great attention to detail. These children are often preoccupied with unusual patterns of objects such as collecting lightbulbs or have a fascination with fire trucks and their specific features, mechanical objects with additional parts, or trains and train schedules. Some children may become experts in specific content areas or areas of interest, learning and being able to repeat various details about historical events, dinosaurs, or airplanes. This high level of attention to detail can make it difficult for children identified with a spectrum disorder to stop a task before it is completed or abruptly close a task on their own time because they become so engrossed in their knowledge base that they become very reluctant to leave it. Children I have met have exhibited atypical movements and high levels of self-stimulating behaviors, such as rocking, flapping the hands, staring at one's fingers, or jumping. Reasons for these behaviors might include self-calming practices, displays of excitement, motor overflow, or uncontrolled, involuntary actions.

Sensory Sensitivities

Although not included as diagnostic criteria for an autism spectrum disorder, many children I have taught exhibited sensory sensitivities in some or all sensory domains, such as strong food preferences that sharply curtail the variety of foods they are willing and able to eat. These children also exhibited hypo- and hypersensitivity to touch and tactile stimulation, sound, light, and glare. For example, it took years of expanding language development and self-awareness before a young adult male with a history of chewing the necklines of his T-shirts was able to tell his mother that the neckline gave him a choking sensation. Once the mother replaced the crewneck style with a V-neck T-shirt, the behavior immediately stopped.

I also observed sensitivities and preferences to smells. For example, hairsprays, colognes, perfumes, chewing gum, and coffee breath could present as aversive to a child with a-spectrum disorder. This same child may not have the language necessary to advocate for removal of an offending odor but may show signs of being bothered by it. Loud noises in the cafeteria or auditorium could be intolerable, requiring the child to wear noise-canceling headsets or making other accommodations to lessen the noise level in such environments.

Children with Spectrum Disorders in the Classroom

Today, evidence-based practices related to autism and those identified on the autism spectrum are prevalent in many programs and interventions. Over the decades many strategies and methodologies have entered the field of education, and most children diagnosed with a spectrum disorder receive either individual or small-group instruction to help them understand their developmental differences, interactions (or noninteractions) with others, and develop communication skills. Quality early intervention is available and critical. As an effective special education teacher, I had to be aware of the many factors and traits that can impact a child's functioning within the school building and beyond.

I ultimately learned that one of the simplest ways to identify a child with the spectrum disorder is to observe the school playground during recess. The solitary child walking around the periphery is likely the candidate. It is a fascinating endeavor for a teacher to truly understand how a student with ASD thinks and why he may behave the way he does. I was always grateful when teacher aides and paraprofessionals were offered professional development sessions where ideas on how to engage, exchange, and promote positive interactions with other students on the playground can be learned. Otherwise, behavioral incident after behavioral incident can result in the school developing a thick dossier on ASD children unless each incident is used to teach replacement behaviors rather than continue reprimanding.

One such example involved a middle schooler who struck a fellow student after observing him stepping on the toes of a female friend. While the lady in distress may have objected loudly, she likely also encouraged the negative interaction. Failing to understand this situation in the context of typical teenage hallway interaction, the student with ASD heard "a damsel in distress" and acted in a manner he thought was justified. Failure of the teacher to understand the entire context of the interaction and those individuals involved yielded the "chivalrous knight" a suspension. This is a good example of how role playing and teaching lessons on social skills are a means of helping an ASD student understand the unwritten rules of life, how to act and react appropriately in particular confrontations, and how to advocate for their firm beliefs in challenging situations like this one. Further, it is equally important that the teacher understands unique behaviors and cognitive processes of ASD children to possibly anticipate a negative student-to-student interaction and react accordingly.

Some children diagnosed with ASD make up words or ascribe alternate meanings to words. It took many months of hearing "Clum, Clum" (referenced earlier in this chapter) before I realized these nonsensical words were the nascent merger of language and the social skill of greeting. A conversation may be initiated by a child in his or her own way. Or a child may prefer to discuss any number of topics with another individual. For example, a teenager with an interest in making a social connection with me once picked up a jar of mustard and began reading the nutrition facts from the label. He did so while maintaining appropriate proximity and eye contact with me, an act appropriate in conversation. If that is what is offered, have a mustard conversation. You may never select mustard as a go-to topic, but if your student finds it of interest, you now have a launch pad for practice in pragmatic language.

A teacher can expect a child with an ASD diagnosis to lack social filters and comment openly and honestly in both positive and negative ways about facial features, hairdo, weight, or wardrobe. Whereas a young child might not understand the concept of possibly hurting someone's feelings when being brutally honest, a teaching opportunity exists for an older child diagnosed with ASD, informing them that such statements, while accurate, would be best left unsaid. Often children diagnosed with ASD are viewed as rude when they don't see the harm in speaking the truth as they perceive it. As these children gain more social experiences, these "unwritten rules" become part of their social repertoire.

Language is often taken literally by children diagnosed with ASD. When using idioms, teachers should explain their meaning. A comment made by a physical education teacher to his special education class to "listen up" resulted in most of the children staring at the gym ceiling. Other examples such as "hold your horses," "catch my drift," or "knock it off" need a simple explanation for children diagnosed with ASD to fully understand the true meaning behind the phrase. Nothing will empower your students more than giving them an understanding of the meaning of language.

Regardless of the level of language understanding of your students, teachers should speak slowly, use concrete terms, and allow time for the child to process what he is hearing. Whether a third grader uses a vocabulary word such as "shimmer" or approximates the word "fish" by saying "ish," the classroom is a minute-by-minute language learning lab. Visuals can assist a child in understanding how to initiate a greeting or end a conversation. "DO" statements are more effective than STOP statements, such as, "put the pencil down" versus "stop playing with the pencil." Often when working with young children, food is used to help the child concretely associate a word and what it represents. The more connections and concepts the child with ASD makes, the more likely he will be able to incorporate meaningful language into his daily life.

Teachers and educational staff who work with children diagnosed with ASD may want to guard their body language, too. Your best hands on hips or facial grimace will likely be lost on a child with ASD unless you instruct him on exactly what it means when you take that physical stance. Social and/or verbal praise may not be as effective as an object, such as a star or picture, given to the young child with diagnosed ASD as his reward. Adolescence can be a particularly challenging time for a teen who has not been taught a functional set of social skills and understanding of various human body language stances. Failing to understand social mores and exactly what constitutes a friendship can often lead an adolescent into misreading body language cues and engaging in inappropriate actions with another teen or adult.

In the classroom, teachers must signal in advance when a transition is coming. The use of individual schedules will help the child or teen diagnosed with ASD to understand the passage of time and visually alert her to an upcoming change or transition. Teachers must understand levels of behavioral and/or verbal prompting and be able to choose the correct one(s) for each child. Verbal prompting is far more conducive to independent functioning, but many ASD children require gestures, modeling, partial physical, or physical prompts to learn and progress.

Stereotypical, repetitive movements ought to be encouraged during a child's free time and after he has completed the task at hand. These behaviors differ from the maladaptive behavior that can be exhibited by ASD children. Such emotional dysregulation is a poorly regulated emotional response that can cause negative emotional reactions and sometimes behavior that mimics "acting out." The fields of psychology and special education have come a long way in identifying what motivates human behavior. These fields now have devised behavior assessments and interventions when teaching replacement behaviors with students diagnosed with ASD. Many decades ago, punishment might have been the only suggested way to correct maladaptive behavior. Today, many different skills and strategies are employed to replace these challenging and interfering behaviors. Some examples include relaxation training, problem-solving skills, strategies for learning how to accept making a mistake, asking for help, and self-calming techniques. It is vital that each child diagnosed with ASD learn self-control, a key strategy to regulating behavior.

As children diagnosed with ASD begin to enter puberty, teachers should keep in mind that parental fears and worries are compounded. As physical appearance, strength, and size transform without a commensurate growth in language, cognition, or adaptive behavior, parents are faced with a whole new set of challenges. Teachers should strive to develop strong, enduring, partnerships with the parents of their students. Over the years, the organization and advocacy of parents of children diagnosed with ASD created the Autism

Society of America, Autism Speaks, the Autism Research Institute, Autism Key, and the National Autism Association among many other organizations. Where possible, school districts ought to offer ongoing parent education and outreach, home interventions, and opportunities for families to share the new challenges they face. Transition and personal futures planning became paramount with a need for the family to focus on vocational training, adult service agencies, living arrangements, trusts, guardianship, Medicaid, and many other adult-oriented considerations. Decades ago, it was the parents who advocated for housing options such as group homes for adult children diagnosed with ASD. These same parents are now advancing the concept of supported homes and apartments and continuing to pave an appropriate path for their children to thrive.

Adolescence is a particularly difficult and painful time for parents of children diagnosed with ASD. Earlier in the child's life and at the beginning of the special education journey, parents may be in a state of denial and cherish the desire for a miracle. It is rather common in the field of ASD for a new medication, treatment, intervention, strategy, or service to be embraced as the newest panacea. With learned strategies, however, acceptance and resolve can keep hope alive and emphasis can be placed on focusing attention on a long-range goal. That goal is to help each individual diagnosed with ASD to reach his full potential regardless of the numerous impediments that a spectrum disorder presents. It is best to be reminded as teachers to "walk a mile in a parents' shoes."

LEGACY

Today, the Centers for Disease Control (CDC) considers the prevalence children diagnosed with ASD as 1 in 44. Autism and ASDs are far more common in males than females, and it is now recognized as a lifelong disability. Given the paucity of children diagnosed early on with a spectrum disorder, the generation of baby-boomer educators eventually forged a path of behavioral interventions and successful teaching strategies. Any gains were attained both through trial and error and through focused, ongoing research, despite insignificant numbers of diagnosed children or current research. The internet and its near instantaneous dissemination of information did not exist to facilitate and share techniques, lesson plans, and methodology among this growing community of children, parents, educators, and researchers. The contrast between evidence-based best practices in use today and the trial-and-error methods of yesteryear is separated by decades of progress. Reflecting on my years working with such children, I realize that we not only benefited from the research but also contributed to it.

The field of special education has come a long way since I first entered the profession more than 50 years ago; so, too, has our understanding of the autism spectrum. The movie *Rain Man*, released in 1988, introduced the layman to autism. Over the years, terminology has changed to afford more dignity to individuals diagnosed with disabilities. Science and research have advanced our understanding of the spectrum, and early infant stimulation programs are available as soon as a baby can be diagnosed. State and national education law protect the child from discrimination and withholding of services. An array of related services is now available for all children with disabilities. Recalling all the children I met along the way, I am grateful for that.

How were special educators able to list, understand, and attempt to address the dozens and dozens of traits and idiosyncratic characteristics of children with ASDs? Ongoing clinical observation and studies were added as steps taken to achieve a proper diagnosis over time. So, too, was the priceless insight of mothers who gave their perspective on raising atypical children as well as adults with ASD who shared their life story through their books and appearances at national and local conferences. I know that the understanding I gained through hearing personal stories was enlightening, encouraging, and vital to my helping their children.

My understanding of the autism spectrum evolved and expanded simultaneously as the academics and clinicians advanced their research. This is my advice for teachers today: Stay aware of the research that focuses on your students; updated information eventually trickles down into the classroom. Aside from trying to understand the unique characteristics of each child diagnosed with ASD, the challenge for today's teachers is to master as many strategies as possible and apply them to meet the diverse, individualized needs of their students. Acquiring a broad knowledge base is demanding, time consuming, and overwhelming. Yet, acquiring this critical skill set will ensure student success. Hopefully, the current cadre of teachers is equipped with the knowledge of the many widely known evidence-based methods, strategies, treatments, and interventions currently available for children diagnosed with ASD and can implement them into their classrooms. I learned as I grew into my identity as a teacher.

Children diagnosed with a spectrum disorder present their own sets of idiosyncrasies, strengths, and preferences when navigating and interacting with the world. Understanding these characteristics will help support academic and social success for students and be very helpful in designing motivational strategies and positive learning environments. Committed teachers must quickly learn to become advocates for their students, working on their behalf for fuller acceptance and integration into school life and society at large.

Teaching in the field of special education is challenging and extremely rewarding. We are all lifelong learners, including individuals with spectrum disorders. I can recall in vivid detail year after year of interesting, challenging, endearing, and determined students who graced my classroom. Their parents, too, left lasting impressions. I found that the more engaged a family is in implementing effective strategies for children diagnosed with ASD, the better the outcome for everyone involved. Each experience with these amazing individuals adds new insight, discovery, and renewed dedication for those of us in the field. One must be willing to accept small triumphs over long periods of time. But continuing to explore, learn, and conduct research on autism, ASDs, and individuals with disabilities carries the torch of John F. Kennedy's legacy speech and gives the children, teens, adults, and their families the attention, dignity, and respect they deserve.

REFERENCES

Al-Beltagi, M. (2021). Autism medical comorbidities. *World journal of clinical pediatrics, 10*(3), 15.

American Psychiatric Association. (2014). *Diagnostic and statistical manual of mental disorders*, 4th ed., text rev. https://doi.org/10.1176/appi.books.9780890425787

Careaga, M., Van de Water, J., & Ashwood, P. (2010). *Immune dysfunction in autism: A pathway to treatment.* Retrieved from https://link.springer.com/content/pdf/10.1016/j.nurt.2010.05.003.pdf

Cohmer, S. (2014). *Early infantile autism and refrigerator mother theory (1943–1970).* Embryo Project Encyclopedia. https://embryo.asu.edu/pages/early-infantile-autism-and-refrigerator-mother-theory-1943-1970

Herman, E. (2019). *The autism history project.* Retrieved from https://blogs.uoregon.edu/autismhistoryproject/topics/autism-in-the-dsm/

Maloney, S. E., Rieger, M. A., & Dougherty, J. D. (2013). Identifying essential cell types and circuits in autism spectrum disorders. *International Review of Neurobiology, 113*, 61–96.

Sheet, D. F. (2010). *Autism spectrum disorders.* National Dissemination Center for Children with Disabilities (NICHCY).

Chapter 5

Catalysts for Change
How Policy Changes Disrupted Inequity in STEM Access

Frances R. Spielhagen

Education policy makers struggle with the challenge of educating all students in diverse learning environments while adhering to state and national standards. This has been particularly problematic in mathematics education. Long regarded as key to individual success, reforms in STEM education have taken center stage in the 21st century.

At the turn of the century, in the wake of No Child Left Behind (NCLB), school leaders in a large urban/suburban district examined the trajectory in mathematics for all students, defining algebra as most important and the key component in STEM success. They sought input and analysis from an external evaluator. Those findings prompted school leaders to confront the embedded inequities in their established curricula. They found, not surprisingly, that students of color and/or in low-income areas of the district were indeed being left behind in STEM educational practices and on the mathematical path to success.

As a result of these findings, school leaders revamped the mathematics policy and sought to provide "algebra for all" students in eighth grade. The intention was to reverse disproportionality in high-school mathematics and to increase STEM involvement of all students in the district. Their efforts were sufficiently successful over the past two decades; hence school leaders continue to support the mathematics access policy. This chapter explains how policy change at the administrative level led to greater student success and, almost more important, teacher support for the policy changes, despite hiccups along the way.

The path has not been easy, but it has been largely successful. Due to policy changes initiated over 20 years, more students from all groups in the district are entering and staying in the STEM pipeline. Further examination reveals some notable lapses in the outcomes. Policy makers in the district continue to examine and address the essential concerns of equity and access in STEM through the study of algebra.

A BRIEF HISTORY OF THE PROBLEM

In the early years of the 21st century, the study of algebra, once considered a subject for "academic" or college-bound students, became an avenue for advancement and a means of broadening the composition of STEM classes. Transformed from its elite status to a necessary component of student success, the study of algebra became a key factor in the study of other STEM subjects in high school. If a student did not study algebra by ninth grade, he would not be enrolled in calculus in 12th grade, and consequently, he was less likely to enroll in STEM courses in college. Robert Moses, founder of the Algebra Project, has long maintained that, ultimately, the study of algebra becomes the lynchpin in future academic and economic success.

Nevertheless, the endorsement in 2008 by the National Mathematics Advisory Panel of the study of algebra as a cornerstone of mathematics for all "prepared" students garnered enough criticism among policy researchers to warrant an entire issue of *Educational Researcher* (December 2008). The core of this outcry was captured in Boaler's (2006) acknowledgment of the extensive range and variety of students in typical mathematics classes, a drastic change from the earliest days of education in the United States.

In the early days, algebra was part of the traditional American grammar school curriculum available to all students as they progressed individually through the grades. Students studied algebra when they got to it in the normal course of the curriculum, very often before entering high school. The conventional curriculum was straightforward, and teachers provided instruction in the various subjects, particularly mathematics, when the students were ready for the topics that flowed from the study before. The environment of small schools allowed teachers to differentiate by simply meeting the immediate needs of the individual students. As a result, some students studied algebra in eighth grade.

However, this changed in the mid-18th to early-20th century when the large influx of students from Europe and the southern U.S. states poured into urban environments. School districts questioned which students should study algebra. This population swell transformed the delivery of curriculum into a lock-step design that policymakers felt would meet the varying educational needs and employment prospects of this vast range of students. Those who might pursue science and engineering certainly would need to study algebra, but those who were not expected to "need" algebra were not given the opportunity to study it.

Although the comprehensive high school became an important link between public elementary school and the state-supported college or university, this path was not open to all students. Students advanced from the grammar school to the high school based on their presumed needs, interests, and ability. In the early 20th century, less affluent students left the educational pipeline after grammar school and, therefore, did not "need" to study algebra. Regardless of whether they could or could not understand algebra, students not planning to go to high school were not given the opportunity to study algebra.

Algebra became the next step in one's education, a step that led to further academic study in mathematics and science and the gateway to educational and employment opportunities beyond high school. Consequently, algebra became the domain of the wealthy. More affluent students were likely to advance to high school and more likely to attend college. Therefore, they "needed" to study algebra to be successful at higher education levels.

This situation became more acute when standards were imposed on the high-school admissions process through the creation of admissions tests. By 1855, high-school admissions tests became one of the first systematic attempts to measure academic progress on the vastly diverse and growing population of students, particularly in urban areas. These tests ultimately became a sorting mechanism that laid the foundation for the inequities that would be challenged a century later.

Prior to these external admissions tests, teachers in typically one-room schools relied on holistic appraisal rubrics. In the quest for predictability in education outcomes, education policy makers considered such holistic measures as inadequate and antiquated. As a result, the first standardized high-school admissions tests emerged as a means of measurement but also of control.

The impetus for this initial standards-based reform movement was to employ high-school admissions tests as a tool for raising standards in public schools (Cremin, 1980), but those standards also changed the curriculum of the grammar schools. Increased numbers of students began to take the admissions tests. To succeed on them, students had to master grammar-school subjects, basically the "three Rs," reading, writing, and arithmetic, but not algebra. Ultimately the high-school admissions tests removed "advanced" subjects such as algebra and Latin from the grammar-school curriculum. They became the domain of the high school.

How did that happen? Because students were not required to answer test items related to algebra on the high-school admissions tests, it became unnecessary to study algebra before entering high school. In effect, the standards for eighth-grade students had been lowered. Prior to the high-school admissions tests, non-college-bound students might have studied algebra in the old grammar-school curriculum. With the new testing system, students not pursuing higher levels of learning lacked algebra accessibility.

More than 40 years ago, as the baby boomers began to assume roles of influence on the American educational landscape, Cremin (1980) decried the discrimination that resulted from the removal of the study of algebra from the grammar-school curriculum in the early 20th century.

> The elimination of advanced subjects below the high school meant lost opportunities for pupils unable to advance. Most high school pupils were from the middle and upper classes; thus, removing advanced subjects from grammar schools restricted chances for the talented but less advantaged youth to taste the higher learning. (p. 154)

Of course, this institutionalized inequity was not a secret. Unwarranted assumptions regarding a student's educational trajectory became the basis of the civil rights movement and the foundation of critical race theory. Robert Moss, a pioneer in the mid-20th century civil rights movement who died in 2021, targeted algebra as a civil right and the key to advanced STEM studies because "in today's world, economic access and full citizenship depend crucially on math and science literacy" (Moses & Cobb, 2001, p. 5). Citing the disturbing statistics that in 1995, blacks comprised only 2.1% of the PhDs in engineering, 1.8% in computer science, and 0.6% in mathematics, Moss maintained that the reorganization of the mathematics curriculum in the industrial era caused the elite status of the study of algebra to be not only a barrier to college entrance, but also to full citizenship and economic autonomy in the United States.

In the two decades since that report, the situation has not improved nationwide. In April, 2021, the Hechinger report stated that "the proportion of bachelor's degrees in science awarded to Black graduates remained flat at about 9 percent from 2001 to 2016, according to the most recent available figures from the National Science Foundation; in engineering, it declined from 5 percent to 4 percent; and in math, it dropped from 7 percent to 4 percent" (Newsom, 2021). Central to this problem is the study of algebra before high school. One student lamented, "I was doing algebra I in high school when my friends who went to the magnet school were taking algebra II, trigonometry, and one was already doing pre-calc. By the time I got to the University of Maryland, I was already two steps behind in math" (Newsom, 2021).

While making its deliberations about the status of algebra in the mathematics curriculum, the National Mathematics Advisory Panel discussed the study of algebra as the foundation for all mathematics and science (Bass, 2006). However, deep within the collective understanding of some American educators resides the opinion that students must have a "rare, innate, ability . . . the math gene" (NACME, 1996, p. 4) to learn algebra and that this ability is possessed only by a select few. The district that faced this problem head-on laid the foundation for opening the doors to STEM study and algebra for all its students, regardless of ethnicity or economic status.

THE SOLUTION

In the face of this ongoing debate regarding mathematics instruction and access and in the absence of a cohesive national initiative, school leaders in a large school district (N = 60,000 students) in the southeastern United States courageously responded to the varied recommendations from NCTM (2000, 2008) and the National Mathematics Advisory Panel (2008). Over several years and into the third decade of the 21st century, these leaders have collaboratively and successfully revamped their district's mathematics policy, and the district now provides algebra instruction in some form for all its students by the eighth grade. The majority of students study algebra in eighth grade or before eighth grade, while a small percentage of students start their study of algebra in eighth grade and continue it into ninth grade. Lessons can be learned in the steps this school district took to change its mathematics policy, its bold decision to establish an eighth-grade "algebra for all" policy, and the outcome of closing the opportunity gap for its diverse student population.

How did this school district bring about such a drastic change in "business as usual"? Over a period of eight years, school leaders worked closely with an outside evaluator who conducted annual reviews of their data. The leaders employed the annual reports to shape and refine their mathematics policy and conducted internal analysis of available data to compare with the evaluator's results. That evaluator conducted both quantitative data analysis and qualitative interviews. Ultimately, school leaders used these data to change the established mathematics delivery policy and how they structured a comprehensive reform that effectively changed the faces of the students sitting in eighth-grade algebra classes. In fact, after eight years of restructuring, more than 90% of the students in the district study algebra at least by eighth grade, and 97% of them pass the state algebra examination.

CHANGING THE GAME BY CHANGING THE PLAYING FIELD

In 2008, the National Mathematics Advisory Panel recommended, "All school districts should ensure that all prepared students should have access to an authentic algebra course—and should prepare more students than at present to enroll in such a course by Grade 8" (p. 23). However, eight years before this important policy statement, school leaders in this district initiated a reform targeting the inherent inequities in their established mathematics delivery policy. Similar to other school districts across the nation, the district serves students who live in an area of approximately 450 square miles. Two-thirds of the population of 300,000 is white or Caucasian/European, approximately one-third is black or African American, and a small percentage (about 3%) is "other," mixed Asian, Hispanic, or Native American.

Like many districts across the nation, long-standing tracking policies had institutionalized inequity in the paths students followed in studying mathematics. Through a complicated system of test scores, course grades, and teacher nominations, some students studied algebra in eighth grade but others did not. Quantitative evidence revealed the disproportionality of algebra access among black students, especially males (Spielhagen, 2006) and of the long-term effects of having eighth-grade algebra (Spielhagen, 2007) under the original protocol for algebra access. Table 1 shows the link between socioeconomic status (SES), as indicated by free and reduced lunch, and access to eighth-grade algebra prior to the reform. In general, school leaders learned that the lower the SES of the school population, the lower the percentage of students studying algebra in eighth grade.

Examination of the composition of the eighth- and ninth-grade algebra classes revealed disproportionality of enrollment of black students in eighth-grade algebra as related to their presence in the general school population. Figures 1 and 2 illustrate the population trends in the two courses.

Further evidence emerged when the leaders examined advanced mathematics course-taking and college enrollment related to having studied algebra in eighth grade. Figures 3 and 4 illustrate the disparities that resulted from restricting access to studying algebra in eighth grade.

EARLY PROGRESS = FOUNDATION FOR SUCCESS

This evidence prompted school leaders to change the algebra delivery policy, reorganize mathematics curricula, increase professional development, and increase student learning supports to ensure that almost all students study

Table 5.1. Course-Taking patterns by Schools: Grade 8 Algebra I versus Grade 9 Algebra 1

School No.	Percent Free/ Reduced Lunch	Grade 8 Algebra I	Grade 9 Algebra I	Ratio Gr. 8 v. Gr. 9
Total		N = 1441	N = 2224	1.54
1	.1%	207	182	.88
2	.2%	173	178	1.03
3	.6%	217	165	.76
4	.9%	143	310	2.17
5	11.8%	92	136	1.48
6	18.4%	123	191	1.55
7	18.9%	139	194	1.40
8	19.4%	108	257	2.38
9	22.4%	122	209	1.71
10	27.3%	36	130	3.61
11	40%	66	245	3.73

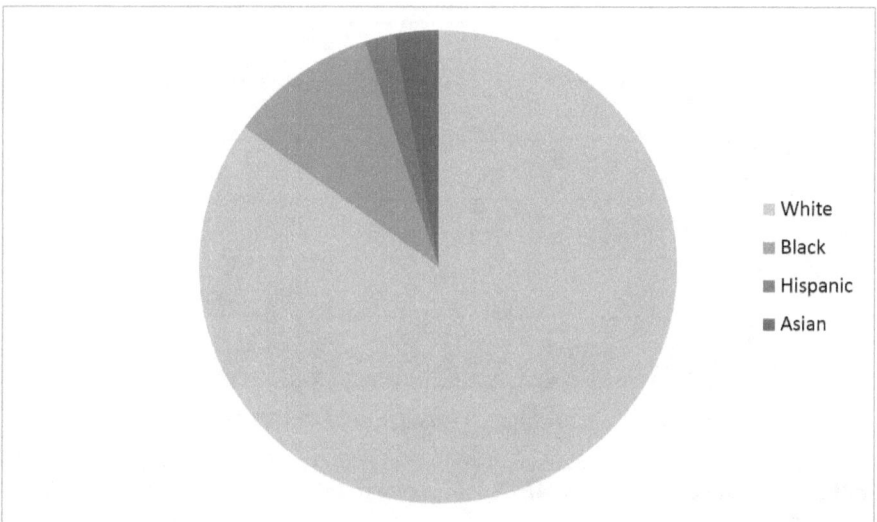

Figure 5.1. Original eighth-grade Algebra I enrollment by ethnicity. *Research is by author using state data, under AERA Postdoctoral Fellowship Protocols. Identities of school district and state are confidential.*

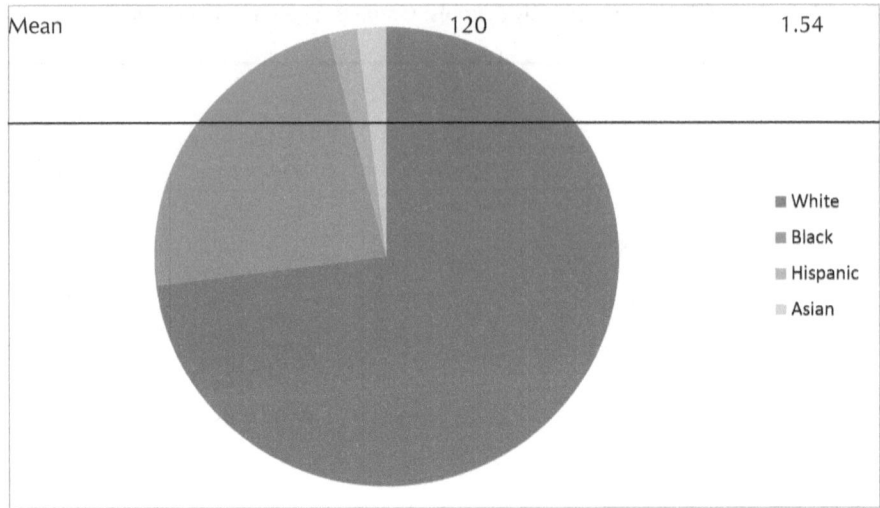

Figure 5.2. Original ninth-grade Algebra I enrollment by ethnicity. *Research is by author using state data, under AERA Postdoctoral Fellowship Protocols. Identities of school district and state are confidential.*

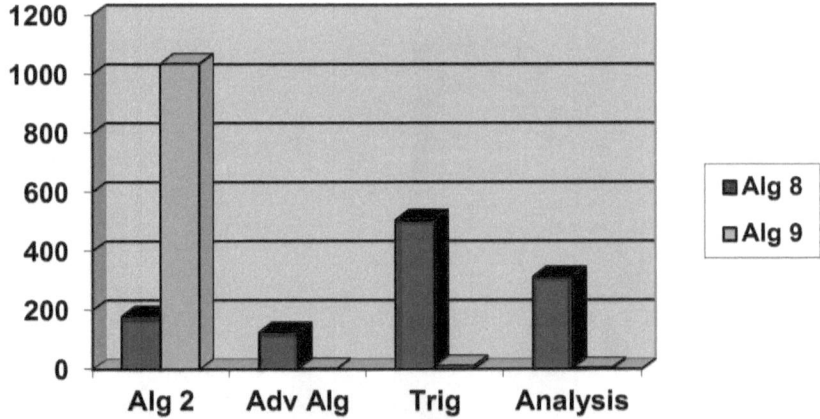

Figure 5.3. Eleventh-grade mathematics course taking after Algebra I. *Research is by author using state data, under AERA Postdoctoral Fellowship Protocols. Identities of school district and state are confidential.*

algebra at least by eighth grade. Gradually but consistently, the schools opened the access to eighth-grade algebra to larger numbers of students, steadily increasing the number of students in the eighth-grade algebra classes each year.

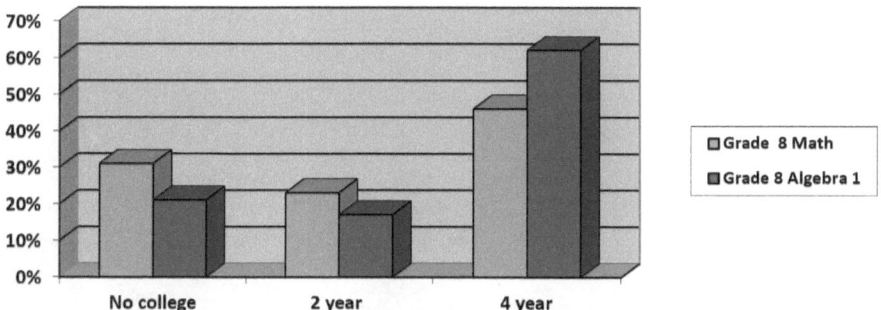

Figure 5.4. College attendance by access to eighth-grade Algebra I. *Research is by author using state data, under AERA Postdoctoral Fellowship Protocols. Identities of school district and state are confidential.*

School leaders in this district embarked on a long, diligent process that involved rigorous reflection at all levels, from the classroom teachers to the superintendent. They implemented consistent policy changes gradually and supported all personnel as well as the students. Student support was critical and involved after-school tutoring sessions as well as differentiation of curriculum to meet the needs of the diverse population. Figure 5 illustrates the gradual change in enrollment in eighth-grade algebra as the district moved steadily toward a successful program of eighth-grade algebra for all but students with the greatest disabilities, from 2005 through 2009.

After eight years of working toward this goal, even among those students who cover the algebra curriculum over two years (starting in eighth grade and finishing in ninth grade), the vast majority of students in this district successfully passed the state's Algebra I examination (Spielhagen, 2011). Among all eighth-grade algebra students, 92% passed the state algebra test, ranking among other students across the state who were in ninth grade. Figure 6 shows the pass rates among eighth-grade students in this district in 2009; figure 7 illustrates the changes in "advanced" pass rate on the same Algebra I test from 2005 to 2009.

These initial pass rates were encouraging to school leaders and laid the foundation for further development of the new policy. Over the years that followed, teachers struggled with addressing the "readiness" of more diverse student populations in algebra courses than they had encountered in prior years. With ongoing professional development and support, they continue to address the needs of the students they now have, rather than pine for the romantic images of students they had before.

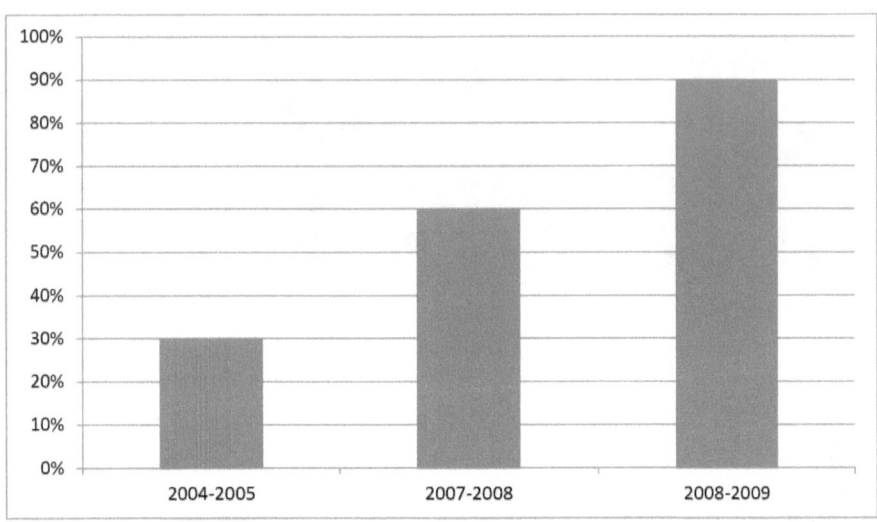

Figure 5.5. Changes in Algebra I enrollment, 2005–2009. *Research is by author using state data, under AERA Postdoctoral Fellowship Protocols. Identities of school district and state are confidential.*

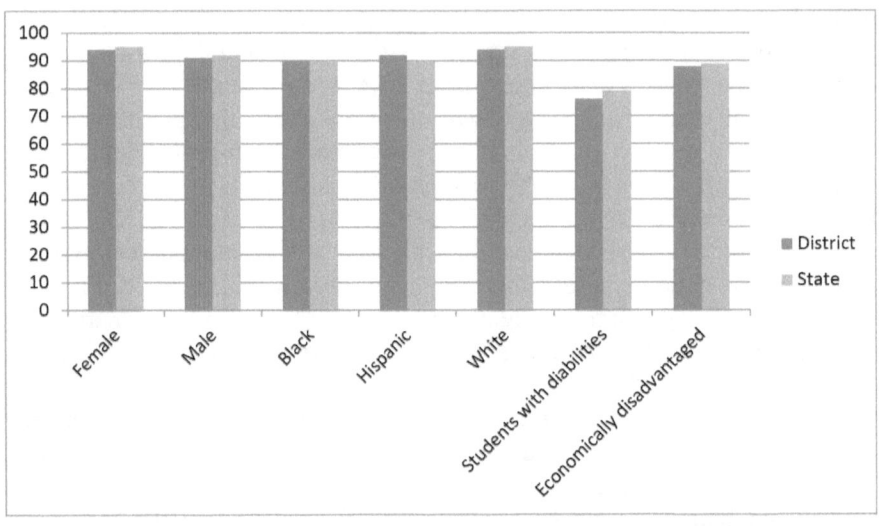

Figure 5.6. Passing rates by demographics. *Research is by author using state data, under AERA Postdoctoral Fellowship Protocols. Identities of school district and state are confidential.*

HOW THEY DID IT: THE COMPONENTS OF SUCCESS

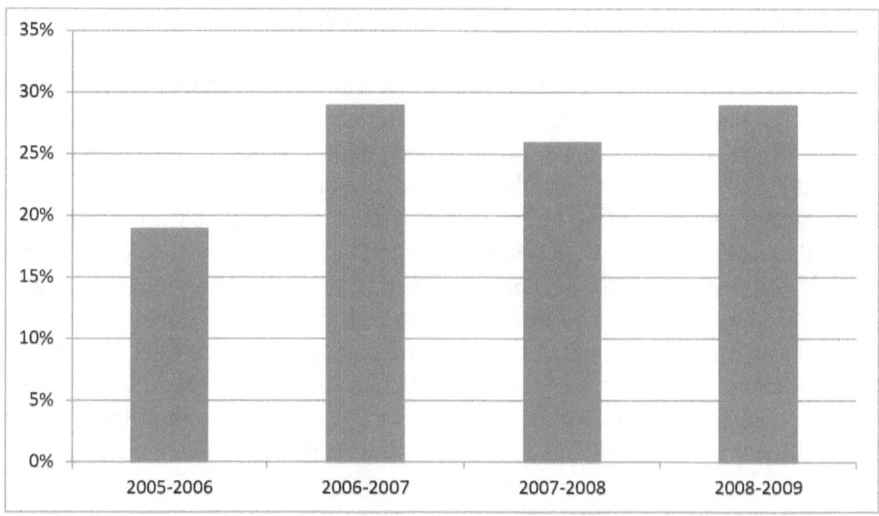

Figure 5.7. Advanced pass rates on state Algebra I test, 2005–2009. *Research is by author using state data, under AERA Postdoctoral Fellowship Protocols. Identities of school district and state are confidential.*

Foolishly, there existed a great deal of backlash to this program change. Much of the criticism stemmed from decreasing the academic level of the established curriculum to give it the name "algebra." An outspoken and vocal critic of eighth-grade algebra programs, Tom Loveless (2008) suggests key elements for algebra programs that he has termed "realistic" (pp. 12–13). Despite his criticism, the elements provide a structure for analyzing the success of algebra programs in this district.

First and most important, student focus should be on learning, not on completing a course. Algebra program initiatives, whether they target eighth- or ninth-grade students, fail because the algebra credential is the goal, not the requisite learning. This district established several structures that fostered learning as the goal. Success followed the focus on learning. Second and equally importantly, the mathematics coordinator and school administrators increased time on task in mathematics throughout the intermediate grades.

In addition, professional development is critically important. The teachers were shown how to differentiate curriculum to meet the varying needs and styles of their diverse populations. No longer was algebra considered the right and domain of certain groups of students—that is, those expected to attend college. If everyone (or most students) was expected to study algebra in eighth grade, then instruction was arranged to make that instruction accessible to all students. One teacher proudly explained, "We teach here," disparaging other environments where only certain elite students are allowed to study algebra in eighth grade.

It is essential that schools teach and assess prerequisite skills and focus on elementary mathematics leading to algebra. The earliest stages of this reform involved professional development for third- and-fourth grade teachers in this district. It is no secret that many teachers in the elementary grades across the United States are "generalists," with little special training and background in mathematics. In fact, the common fear is that many of these teachers are also math phobic. By providing targeted professional development in the algebra skills that derive from instruction in the intermediate grades, the school leaders laid the foundation for success for these students in eighth-grade algebra.

At the same time, engage in early intervention. Build an infrastructure for all students leading to eighth grade. Admittedly, for some teachers in this district, the concept of "readiness" was a difficult stumbling block to implementing eighth-grade algebra for all. At each step, teachers expressed fears about the readiness of their students to handle more complex concepts.

However, readiness may be defined in many ways, and it is a catch-all word that can be exclusive rather than inclusive. Gradually, as they continued their own professional development, the teachers realized that they were equating readiness with resources, and that, for some students, the teachers may be their best, if not only, resource. As a result, after-school and lunchtime tutoring programs began to emerge throughout the district, while in some parts of the district, parents themselves provided private tutoring. The focus was on success in learning. It is no surprise that "readiness" continues to plague this district's efforts to maintain this equitable change in curriculum.

Finally, it is imperative that school districts collect data and conduct their own research so that they can examine the results of what they are doing. This step is critically important so that light can be shed on latent structures feeding inequity. Although this district worked with an outside evaluator in the early stages of the reform, leaders continued their own analysis over the subsequent two decades.

At every step, school leaders asked good questions, took their findings into consideration, and implemented district-wide reform over the next five years. As a result, this district turned around mathematics achievement for its students. Whereas only 30.7% of the district's eighth-grade students were enrolled in algebra in 2004–2005, effectively 90% of the eighth graders were studying algebra in the 2008–2009 school year, a percentage that has continued into 2022.

Moreover, in this increased pool of eighth-grade algebra course takers, 92% passed the state's Algebra 1 examination, scoring a bit lower than the state average (94%) that includes students studying algebra in ninth grade. Even more powerful are the results for various subgroups within the eighth-grade population studying Algebra I. In every group, students scored comparably with the other test takers in the state, even though the larger sample included students who were studying algebra in the ninth grade. The extra year of mathematics preparation did not seem to make an appreciable difference in the test scores.

Admittedly, the high passing scores on the state algebra test may indicate a larger problem of the rigor of the test. Nevertheless, the fact remains that on the state measure, the eighth-grade students in this district scores comparably when compared to others in the larger population across the state. As long as state tests are a universally accepted measure of student success, then these results are worth consideration. Moreover, district administrators are not content with passing scores. They have been following the "advanced pass rate" among their students taking the state Algebra I test, and that also increased steadily since they have implemented the eighth-grade algebra policy. Across this state, other districts have followed suit and implemented eighth-grade algebra policies.

In the years since full implementation of the algebra for all initiative, eighth-grade Algebra I enrollment patterns increased, and the opportunity to take Algebra I in eighth grade yielded expanded opportunities for students to enroll in five or more credit-bearing mathematics courses before they graduate. In these two measures, the algebra for all initiative has had a positive impact.

However, the algebra for all initiative did not seem to have the same positive impact on students with disabilities and economically disadvantaged students. The success gap, which compares student participation data with student success data, suggests that although all students may be enrolling in Algebra I at a greater rate, not all students are meeting success in Algebra I equally. Nevertheless, in terms of equity of opportunity, this study suggests that the algebra for all initiative has had a sustained, positive impact.

ACCESSIBILITY: THE KEY TO EQUITY

Much has been said about achievement gaps in the United States, particularly in mathematics. On international test reports such as the PISA (Program for International Student Assessment), students in the United States score dismally in mathematics in comparison with their peers across the globe. In response to these reports, pundits frequently cite the problems inherent in teaching all students in a democracy and the unavoidable socioeconomic differences in resources among student populations, especially among those from lower socioeconomic environments. However, little has been said about the opportunity gaps that exist in some districts, particularly those with limited financial resources and low-income populations.

Raudenbush, Fotiu, and Cheoung (1998) targeted the issue of access of minority students to the study of algebra and found that more affluent districts were more likely to provide algebra instruction to students in eighth grade than districts with fewer financial resources. Their results indicate "substantial evidence of inequality of access to these resources as a function of social background and ethnicity" (p. 265). Smith (1996) also found that "early algebra takers were less likely to be from minority groups and came from families of higher socioeconomic status" (p. 145). Fueled by equity and civil rights initiatives of the mid-20th century, these studies paved the way for the initiative undertaken by this district and its subsequent success in algebra access for all students.

This is not an easy path. It remains the task of the school to address the needs of its student population in ways that are inclusive and foster academic success. Punitive, exclusive programming makes it difficult, if not impossible, for students of diverse backgrounds to access and progress along a continuum of academic growth. Similarly, tracking policies that sort students early in their academic careers are also impediments to accessibility. Policies that include inclusivity and access allowed this school district the ability to allow for individual algebra development and growth, provide smooth transitions in mathematics instruction for all students, and consider success as incremental experiences rather than a set of hurdles or insurmountable steps as roadblocks.

Access to eighth-grade algebra can best be understood in the spirit of how architects now provide access to buildings in the United States. Where once all buildings were entered by means of stairs, steps, if you will, now there are ramps. These ramps lead to entrances and provide open access for all to approach the building under their own steam, with help if necessary. Gradual access is provided for all, from those who proceed quickly and race to the top to those who move more slowly, with accommodations such as wheelchairs and walkers. No physical barriers impede the individual's progress up the ramp.

This metaphor defines the success of this school district and its students. Access to eighth-grade algebra is no longer reserved for a select few or those who can "make it to the top" of a series of steep academic steps. Instead, all students in this school district now progress steadily up the ramp to algebra at least by eighth grade. Some get there sooner than others, but the vast majority get there. These school leaders and their students accomplished substantial change in the school culture in their district, providing academic access that all students deserve.

Educators at all levels collaborated to bring about this policy reform. Their efforts can serve as a template for school leaders in other districts who strive to bring about realistic change in this tense era of accountability. Despite hiccups along the way, most teachers are on board with the new plan and take pride in their success rates. In the face of rhetoric about achievement gaps and "racing to the top," school leaders and teachers in this district have closed the opportunity gap for students going into high school and continue to provide a strong foundation for further academic growth. That is no small accomplishment.

LESSONS LEARNED

The commitment of these school district leaders to widening the gates to STEM opportunities was not without difficulty and struggle. In the end, a vision of equity, born out of altruism and idealism, led each player to push forward despite difficulties along the way. Once more, one is reminded of the clarion call of John F. Kennedy to ask what we can do for our country. This district acted on behalf of its students in response to the needs school leaders perceived without waiting for a national mandate.

In the final analysis, these are the key takeaways from this collaboration of a baby-boomer researcher with like-minded school leaders:

1. Good intentions may be clear, but the path to equity is murky and fraught with difficulty. Be prepared realistically for the long haul.
2. Positive change can come from top-down policy mandates, but teachers must be brought into the process. They are the key players in this effort.
3. Changing hearts and minds results from informing those hearts and minds through constant, incremental, professional development. Honor the intelligence and good will of the teachers.
4. Helping some students is better than maintaining the status quo and not helping any. Those who walk through the wider gates serve as role models for those who follow and reference points for teachers.
5. Change is a recursive process, building on the steps that go before. Move forward, always, with the key goal in mind: greater equity for all students.
6. In the words of Winston Churchill, "Never, never give up!"

REFERENCES

American Educational Research Association. (2008). *Educational researcher: Special issue on foundations for success: The final report of the national mathematics advisory panel.* Sage.

Boaler, J. (2006). "Opening our ideas": How a detracked mathematics approach promoted respect, responsibility, and high achievement. *Theory into Practice, 45*(1), 40–46.

Cavanaugh, S. (2008, July 30). Experts question California's algebra edict. *Education Week*. https://www.edweek.org/teaching-learning/experts-question-calif-s-algebra-edict/2008/07

Cremin, L. (1980). *American education: The national experience.* Harper & Row.

Fennell, F. (2008, January/February). What algebra? When? National Council of Teachers of Mathematics. https://www.nctm.org/News-and-Calendar/Messages-from-the-President/Archive/Skip-Fennell/What-Algebra_-When_/

Loveless, T. (2008). *The misplaced math student: Lost in eighth grade algebra.* Brookings Institution.

Moses, B., & Cobb, C. (2000). *Radical equations: Math, literacy, and civil rights.* Beacon Press.

National Council of Teachers of Mathematics. (2000). *Principles and standards for school mathematics.* National Council of Teachers of Mathematics.

National Mathematics Advisory Panel. (2008). *Foundations for success: The final report of the national mathematics advisory panel.* U.S. Department of Education.

Newsome, M. (2021, April 12). *Even as colleges pledge to improve, share of engineering and math graduates who are black declines.* Hechinger Report. https://www.pbs.org/newshour/education/even-as-colleges-pledge-to-improve-share-of-engineering-graduates-who-are-black-declines

Raudenbush, S. W., Fotiu, R. P., & Cheong, Y. F. (1998). Inequality of access to educational resources: A national report card for eighth-grade math. *Educational Evaluation and Policy Analysis, 20*(4), 253–267.

Smith, J. (1996). Does an extra year make any difference? The impact of early access to algebra on long-term gains in mathematics achievement. *Educational Evaluation and Policy Analysis, 18*(2), 141–153.

Spielhagen, F. (2006). Closing the achievement gap in math: Policy implications of eighth grade algebra for all students. *American Secondary Education, 34*(3), 29–42.

Spielhagen, F. (2007). Closing the achievement gap in math: The long-term effects of eighth grade algebra. *Journal for Advanced Academics, 18*(1), 34–59.

Spielhagen, F. (2011). *The algebra solution to mathematics reform: Completing the equation.* Teachers College Press.

Taylor, R. (1990). Teacher expectations of students enrolled in algebra. In E. Edwards (Ed.), *Algebra for everyone* (pp. 45–52). National Council of Teachers of Mathematics.

Chapter 6

Gifted Education and Talent Development
Roots and Wings

Sally M. Reis

National and international events influence educators and the public's interest about identifying, assessing, and developing gifts and talents in young people. Growing up in the 1950s was an essential part of the development of my subsequent career as a scholar and researcher. One technological feat by the former Soviet Union, the launching of Sputnik, forced the United States to examine its educational system, especially in math and science and the education of students with gifts and talents.

THE PROBLEM

The successful launching of Sputnik in 1957 awakened both politicians and educators to a national problem focusing on policies related to developing the talents of young people. What was happening to academically talented students in the United States? Were we considering how to develop talents in the sciences? If so, how were students being identified and served? What should the education goals and outcomes be for this population? In other words, was our country doing enough to challenge academically talented students? Would we fall behind in the race to get to the moon?

Almost two decades later, the Congress of the United States commissioned a report on the status of gifted children. Sidney Marland was the commissioner of education, and in 1972, he summarized information from a national survey study and offered the first federal definition:

Gifted and talented children are those identified by professionally qualified persons who, by virtue of outstanding abilities, are capable of high performance. These are children who require differentiated educational programs and/or services beyond those normally provided by the regular school program to realize their contribution to society. Children capable of high performance include those with demonstrated achievement and/or potential in any of the following areas, singly or in combination:
- general intellectual ability,
- specific academic ability,
- creative or productive thinking,
- leadership ability,
- visual and performing arts, and
- psychomotor ability. (Marland, 1972, p. 2)

The Marland report also indicated that 3 to 5% of the K–12 population could be considered gifted and talented. Although the Marland report opened a critical door for the many students who needed programming beyond what the regular classroom offered, the ways in which the definition was operationalized also inadvertently limited the identification and participation of many more students who would have benefited from the enriched and accelerated learning programs.

A few years later, the 1972 definition was revised, keeping most of the terminology but eliminating psychomotor ability. The revised definition follows from Public Law 95–561:

[The gifted and talented are] children and, whenever applicable, youth who are identified at the pre-school, elementary, or secondary level as possessing demonstrated or potential abilities that give evidence of high performance capability in areas such as intellectual, creative, specific academic or leadership ability or in the performing and visual arts, and who by reason thereof require services or activities not ordinarily provided by the school. (Gifted and Talented Education Act, 1978, p. 150)

In the United States, almost two decades passed before a new federal definition was offered. In 1993, the report titled *National Excellence: A Case for Developing America's Talent* outlined the economic, educational, social, and emotional ramifications of neglecting the development of students' talents and gifts. The resulting definition of children with outstanding talent follows:

Children and youth with outstanding talent perform or show the potential for performing at remarkably high levels of accomplishment when compared with others of their age, experience, or environment.

These children and youth exhibit high performance capability in intellectual, creative, and/or artistic areas, possess an unusual leadership capacity, or excel in specific academic fields. They require services or activities not ordinarily provided by the schools. (Office of Educational Research and Improvement, 1993, p. 26)

Further, "Outstanding talents are present in children and youth from all cultural groups, across all economic strata, and in all areas of human endeavor" (Office of Educational Research and Improvement, 1993, p. 26).

The National Excellence report (1993) uses damning language: "the educational foundations of our society are presently being eroded by a rising tide of mediocrity that threatens our very future as a Nation and a people" (p. 9). Using dire cold war language, the report titled *A Nation at Risk* (National Commission on Excellence in Education, 1983) also famously stated, "If an unfriendly foreign power had attempted to impose on America the mediocre educational performance that exists today, we might well have viewed it as an act of war" (p. 9).

THE SOLUTION: NEW DEFINITIONS AND PROGRAMMING APPROACHES

During this time of the federal interest in defining gifted and talented children and youth or children with outstanding talent, many researchers reflected on giftedness, talents, and intelligences, especially Joseph Renzulli, Howard Gardner, and Robert Sternberg. For example,

Renzulli (1978) offered a research-based definition of giftedness that is widely cited:

> Giftedness consists of an interaction among three basic clusters of human traits—above-average general abilities, high levels of task commitment, and high levels of creativity. Gifted and talented children are those possessing or capable of developing this composite set of traits and applying them to any potentially valuable areas of human performance. Children who manifest or are capable of developing an interaction among these three clusters require a wide variety of educational opportunities and services that are not ordinarily provided through regular instructional programs. (p. 261)

Gardner focused on domains versus human traits in his 1983 theory of multiple intelligences based on the following definition:

> A human intellectual competence must entail a set of skills of problem solving—enabling the individual to *resolve genuine problems or difficulties* that he or she encounters and, when appropriate, to create an effective product—and must also entail the potential for *finding or creating problems*—thereby laying

the groundwork for the acquisition of new knowledge. ("4. INTELLEGENCE 4.1 CONCEPTS AND DEFINITIONS: Intelligence has . . . - AIU") (pp. 60–61)

Gardner identified an original set of seven intelligences that met the specific criteria he established for intelligence, including: linguistic, logical-mathematical, visual spatial, bodily kinesthetic, musical, interpersonal, and intrapersonal. In recent years, Gardner discussed considered the possibility of adding two additional intelligences: naturalist and existential (Gardner & Traub, 1999).

Sternberg was also conducting research on intelligence during this period. Over several decades, Sternberg proposed related theories about the meaning and application of intelligence among cultures of people around the world. His triarchic theory of intelligence (1985) focused on analytical, creative, and practical intelligences:

- Analytical intelligence: Solving familiar problems by using strategies that manipulate elements of a problem;
- Creative intelligence: Solving new kinds of problems that require thinking about the problem in new ways; and
- Practical intelligence: Solving problems that apply what we know to everyday contexts.

A decade later, Sternberg (1999) proposed a newer conception of successful intelligence, suggesting that an individual can achieve success by capitalizing on strengths while systematically adapting, correcting, and capitalizing on weaknesses. Newer definitions also subsequently emerged. The National Association for Gifted Children (NAGC) convened a group of contemporary researchers and practitioners that offered a new definition:

> Gifted individuals are those who demonstrate outstanding levels of aptitude (defined as an exceptional ability to reason and learn) or competence (documented performance or achievement in top 10% or rarer) in one or more domains. Domains include any structured area of activity with its own symbol system (e.g., mathematics, music, language) and/or set of sensorimotor skills (e.g., painting, dance, sports). (National Association for Gifted Children, 2010, para. 1)

In addition, this NAGC definition highlighted the lifelong process of developing abilities or talents, reinforcing how performance and productivity could indicate potentials at different ages.

DEVELOPMENT OF A WIDELY USED ENRICHMENT PROGRAMMING MODEL

From Renzulli's broadened conception of giftedness and his focus on creative productive giftedness, our subsequent work on the development of the schoolwide enrichment model (SEM) emerged, published first in 1985 with two subsequent revisions (Renzulli & Reis, 1985, 1997, 2014). Renzulli's earlier work combined his previously developed enrichment triad model into a broader talent-development approach, a product of four decades of research and field testing (Reis & Peters, 2021). The original enrichment triad model (Renzulli, 1977) was designed to offer enrichment to a broader pool of students in whom we could develop talents. The popularity of that work with Renzulli emerged into the SEM, one of the most widely implemented and used enrichment/gifted education models in the world. The past four decades have been spent developing the SEM, studying its implementation and impact, and traveling across the globe to expand its implementation. The SEM is used in thousands of school districts, and we remain dedicated to the extensive evaluation and research with others who have worked to investigate the utility and effectiveness of the model.

Simply stated, we believe now, as we have over the past four decades in which the SEM has been implemented, that *schools should be places for talent development* (Renzulli, 1994). A talent-development approach must move beyond various iterations of standards-based learning and the current knowledge-based curriculum, no matter how fast and advanced those standards and that curriculum may be. Our SEM talent-development model resists the temptation to standardize students. Our focus in the SEM is on the flexible development of a broad range of thinking skills and an attitudinal focus on and mind-set of creative productivity.

Our research documents how the use of the SEM can result in broader identification procedures of and enrichment services for students from diverse groups and lower socioeconomic backgrounds who are now also included in a SEM talent pool (Reis & Peters, 2021). We have consulted with more than 25 countries and all 50 states on the talent development, enrichment, and differentiation approach described in the SEM.

Research on the Impact of Extending Gifted Education Pedagogy to a Broader Pool of Students

Also based on the work completed on the SEM, an interest emerged about how the pedagogy of the SEM, called enrichment pedagogy, could be used to provide more engaging and interesting learning experiences for all students, an idea that resulted in an online enrichment system called Renzulli learning.

During that time, the first Renzulli Academy was also developed. The academy implemented all components of the SEM, including the related reading study focusing on schoolwide enrichment model in reading as a full and total school enrichment approach. The academy also proved how well urban students with high potential would do in a very different type of school (Reis & Morales-Taylor, 2010). With a very broad pool of students, average and above average in achievement and using enrichment pedagogy, we built a climate and a school known for academics and engagement. The academy students who were not the top scorers in statewide achievement tests in the city became the top test takers in the district without any test preparation. Rather, these students scored well because of their participation in authentic investigations and pursuing enrichment opportunities on a regular basis. Even more important, the academy students won invention convention competitions, history day presentations, and many arts and math awards.

The use of SEM proved to be effective with diverse populations, including students who are twice-exceptional (Baum et al., 2014; Reis, Baum, & Burke, 2014), who underachieve in school (Baum et al., 1995), and who are from culturally and linguistically diverse groups (Beecher & Sweeny, 2008; Reis & Morales-Taylor, 2010). The talent pool identification model and interest-based enrichment provide opportunities for students beyond those who are academically gifted, including for those who have creative-productive potential. This increased exposure, along with opportunities for interest-based activities, was found to increase engagement and opportunities for enriched learning, as well as higher achievement scores (Beecher & Sweeney, 2008).

Talented Readers and the Schoolwide Enrichment Reading Model (SEM-R)

Research has addressed using enrichment strategies to challenge and engage readers of all achievement levels, especially talented readers. This work, titled the *Schoolwide Enrichment Reading Model* or SEM-R, was funded by two large (approximately $6 million) federal grants, and this cutting-edge research has been investigated, replicated, and published in the most competitive educational journals. The major result of this empirical work was that when using SEM-R, teachers could eliminate most of group reading instruction (up to 4–5 hours weekly) and replace it with targeted, differentiated reading instruction applied to interest-based books that students select and want to read. When teachers implemented SEM-R for an academic year, students participating in the SEM-R, as compared to a randomly assigned treatment group, achieved either higher or similar scores on standardized tests of reading fluency and achievement. These results were testimony to the efficacy of enrichment-based reading and differentiated instruction.

This same research group studied the use of enrichment clusters for the entire population of students in two economically disadvantaged, culturally diverse, urban schools (Reis, Gentry, & Maxfield, 1999). Enrichment clusters provide a regularly scheduled time for students and adults who share a common interest and purpose to come together to complete enrichment work. Our research indicates that high-end learning opportunities can extend opportunities for advanced learning to all students in a school. This concept further promotes the positive notion of schoolwide enrichment for all students.

Research on Curriculum Differentiation and Compacting

Another component of the SEM that has been investigated relates to teaching strategies that enable teachers to streamline the regular curriculum, ensure student mastery of basic skills, and provide time for challenging enrichment and/or acceleration activities. This teaching strategy of curriculum compacting, one of the components of the SEM, enables every student in every classroom to be academically challenged. Our research on this topic demonstrates that academically talented students can be compacted out of 40–50% of the regular curriculum in content area such as reading, science, and mathematics without any decrease in their achievement test sores (Reis, Westberg, Kulikowich, & Purcell, 1998).

Research on Gifted Students with Disabilities (Twice-Exceptionality or 2e)

This addresses enrichment and talent development opportunities for these 2e students who have both extreme talents and deficits. Compensation strategies, such as extra time on tests, providing additional instruction of learning strategies, and a variety of deeper processing strategies, help 2e students learn to work smarter in school but don't ignite their interests or passions about learning. Therefore, my research in helping teachers provide both compensation strategies and opportunities for high-level, high-quality enrichment learning opportunities remains a major theme of my professional career and will continue with a new federal grant to study 2e students who are also identified as autistic.

Expanding my research focus on using gifted education strategies to benefit students with disabilities has been an important personal evolution. For example, the research we conducted on the SEM-R was also applied to total school populations. We found that below average readers and readers identified with disabilities also relished the opportunity to select books in which they had an interest and have their instruction differentiated and personalized. And these students did better with far less whole-group instruction than their control group of below average readers who received grouped, regular reading instruction.

In addition, the research conducted on enrichment clusters found that implementing this form of gifted education pedagogy for all students, including a school with more than 90 students identified as having behavior disorders, resulted in higher engagement and enjoyment in school, less absenteeism, and almost no behavioral problems. And why shouldn't students identified with disabilities have opportunities to pursue their interests and learn the strategies they need to succeed in school while also doing creative work in areas of interest and enjoyment?

LESSONS LEARNED

Taken collectively, the research about definitions and programming models has suggested a few important lessons.

First and foremost, research continues to demonstrate that many students identified as academically talented are underachieving in school, potentially due to non-challenging curricula (Reis & McCoach, 2000), and need and deserve to be both identified and served.

Second, a direct relationship should exist between the identification system and the types of services offered in the talent-development program developed for schools. If, for example, the program is designed to provide advanced-level curriculum in math, then math scores and achievement levels in mathematics should be used to identify students and provide programming options. If, on the other hand, a program is developed to respond to individual student interests and encourage creative productivity in students' strength areas, then a logical identification system that assesses their interests, abilities, and creativity should be considered. In other words, the identification system should follow rather than precede the development of program practices.

Next, educational services provided to students should be based on important theories and should be research driven. The definitions and programming practices discussed in this chapter, therefore, should also maintain some integrity to theory and respect for the research that the theory generates. A theory is an organized and integrated set of ideas formed by speculation based on previous knowledge, experience, reflection, observation, and past practice. Theories reflect ideas, purposes, and values deemed important to persons who have developed or adopted a given theory. The most important roles of a theory are, first, to guide a model that affects practical activities taking place in schools, classrooms, and other places where learning occurs; and second, to guide research about the effectiveness of those practices.

When I started my research career, I was influenced, and continue to be, by my years as a public school teacher. Most of the researchers whom I admired the most, including Renzulli, Sternberg, Torrance, and Gallagher, were conducting applied and/or school-based research and beginning to contribute theories with practical application for teachers.

In hindsight, I wish I had arrived earlier at the importance of gifted education pedagogy, schools based on the SEM, and the impact these theories, models, and practices could make for all students. But the time in the intervening decades was most likely necessary because I was able to better understand the power and the importance of these paths.

As education has changed so much, it was most likely essential to better understand that the standards movement that has overtaken American education would have a negative impact on many high potential and gifted students. In reflecting on my career, I benefited from my decades of experience and the funded research opportunities I had to experiment with applications of gifted education pedagogy on all students, including those with disabilities. Understanding that all students should have opportunities to develop their talents and interests has been essential to my development as a scholar over time.

These intellectual ideas, gained over decades of research and practice, have shown that gifted education pedagogy should be driving more educational practices for all students. More students should be given the opportunity to develop their creative potential, to work in areas of interest, to have personalized and differentiated instruction, and to develop their talents. In some schools, the talent pool should be much, much larger, and I have come to believe that more students will be engaged and happy if we consider all students in the talent pool and plan educational experiences around the services in the SEM and SEM-R. Personal interests guide so much of what students do, and those creative accomplishments completed in school can be one of the most important guiding lessons for one's future.

It is critical to continue examining conceptions of human potential and to learn more about how educators can transform students' potential to high-level, creative, productive work. Adopting a talent-development educational framework and implementing intentional opportunities will build the talent base in our schools. Viewing schools as places for talent development (Renzulli & Reis, 2014) will make a difference for students and educators as human potentials are recognized, supported, and developed to meet the contemporary challenges of our world. Just as my own opportunity to complete self-selected, highly creative work in college defined my intellectual journey, more creative work in schools can result in a larger pool of creative, fulfilled adults whose work makes a difference in the world. Perhaps that understanding is also an outgrowth of growing up as a baby boomer and attending college during the 1960s and 1970s.

REFERENCES

Baum, S. M., Renzulli, J. S., & Hébert, T. P. (1995). Reversing underachievement: Creative productivity as a systematic intervention. *Gifted Child Quarterly, 39*(4), 224–235. https://doi.org/10.1177%2F001698629503900406

Baum, S. M., Schader, R. M., & Hébert, T. P. (2014). Through a different lens: Reflecting on a strengths-based, talent-focused approach for twice-exceptional learners. *Gifted Child Quarterly, 58*(4), 311–327. https://doi.org/10.1177/0016986214547632

Beecher, M., & Sweeny, S. M. (2008). Closing the achievement gap with curriculum enrichment and differentiation: One school's story. *Journal of Advanced Academics, 19*(3), 502–530. https://doi.org/10.4219%2Fjaa-2008-815

Education for All Handicapped Children Act (EHA; also known as PL 94–142). (1975). https://www.govinfo.gov/content/pkg/STATUTE-89/pdf/STATUTE-89-Pg773.pdf#page=1

Gardner, H. (1983). *Frames of mind: The theory of multiple intelligences.* Basic Books.

Gardner, H., & Traub, J. (1999). *A debate on "multiple intelligences."* Cerebrum: Dana Foundation. https://dana.org/article/a-debate-on-multiple-intelligences/

Gifted and Talented Children's Education Act, Public Law 95–561. (1978). https://www.govinfo.gov/content/pkg/STATUTE-92/pdf/STATUTE-92-Pg2143.pdf

Jacob K. Javits Gifted and Talented Students Education Act of 2001. Pub. L. 89–10, title V, §5461, as added Pub. L. 107–110, title V, §501, January 8, 2002, 115 Stat. 1826.

Marland, Jr., S. P. (1971). *The Marland report.* Department of Health, Education, and Welfare: Office of Education. https://files.eric.ed.gov/fulltext/ED056243.pdf

National Association for Gifted Children. (2010). *Redefining giftedness for a new century: Shifting the paradigm.* National Association for Gifted Children. https://www.nagc.org/sites/default/files/Position%20Statement/Redefining%20Giftedness%20for%20a%20New%20Century.pdf

Office of Educational Research and Improvement (1993). *National excellence: A case for developing America's talent.* Office of Educational Research and Improvement. https://files.eric.ed.gov/fulltext/ED359743.pdf

Reis, S. M., Baum, S. M., & Burke, E. (2014). An operational definition of twice-exceptional learners: Implications and applications. *Gifted Child Quarterly, 58*(3), 217–230. https://doi.org/10.1177/0016986214534976

Reis, S. M., Gentry, M., & Maxfield, L. R. (1998). The application of enrichment clusters to teachers' classroom practices. *Journal for Education of the Gifted, 21*(3), 310–324.

Reis, S. M., & McCoach, D. B. (2000). The underachievement of gifted students: What do we know and where do we go? *Gifted Child Quarterly, 44*(3), 152–170.

Reis, S. M., McCoach, D. B., Little, C. M., Muller, L. M., & Kaniskan, R. B (2011). The effects of differentiated instruction and enrichment pedagogy on reading achievement in five elementary schools. *American Educational Research Journal, 48*(2), 462–501. https://doi.org/10.3102/0002831210382891

Reis, S. M., & Morales-Taylor, M. (2010). From high potential to gifted performance: Encouraging academically talented urban students. *Gifted Child Today, 33*(4), 28–38.

Reis, S. M., & Peters, P. M. (2021). Research on the Schoolwide Enrichment Model: Four decades of insights, innovation, and evolution. *Gifted Education International, 37*(2), 109–141.

Reis, S. M., Westberg, K. L., Kulikowich, J. M., & Purcell, J. H. (1998). Curriculum compacting and achievement test scores: What does the research say? *Gifted Child Quarterly, 42*, 123–129.

Renzulli, J. S. (1978). What makes giftedness? Reexamining a definition. *Phi Delta Kappan, 60*(3), 180–184, 261. https://www.jstor.org/stable/20299281

Renzulli, J. S. (1994). *Schools for talent development*. Waco, TX: Prufrock Press.

Renzulli, J. S. (1998). The three-ring conception of giftedness. In S. M. Baum, S. M. Reis, & L. R. Maxfield (Eds.), *Nurturing the Gifts and Talents of Primary Grade Students (pp. 1–6)*. Mansfield Center, CT: Creative Learning Press. http://www.gifted.uconn.edu/sem/semart13.html

Renzulli, J. S., & Reis, S. M. (1985). *The Schoolwide Enrichment Model: A comprehensive plan for educational excellence*. Mansfield Center, CT: Creative Learning Press.

Renzulli, J., & Reis, S. (1997). *The Schoolwide Enrichment Model: A how-to guide for educational excellence*, 2nd ed. Mansfield, CT: Creative Learning Press.

Renzulli, J., & Reis, S. (2014). *The Schoolwide Enrichment Model: A how-to guide for educational excellence*, 3rd ed. Waco, TX: Prufrock Press.

Sternberg, R. J. (1985). *Beyond IQ: A triarchic theory of human intelligence*. Cambridge University Press.

Sternberg, R. J. (1999). The theory of successful intelligence. *Review of General Psychology, 3*(4), 292–316. https://doi.org/10.1037/1089-2680.3.4.292

United States. National Commission on Excellence in Education. (1983). *A nation at risk: the imperative for educational reform*. Washington, DC.

Chapter 7

Leadership in Times of Crisis
From First-Generation Student to College President

Steven DiSalvo

The summer of 1969 offered the perfect dichotomy of hope and vision for the future combined with the wounds inflicted by a decade of civil unrest that encapsulated American culture. When I was a young boy, there was much to celebrate as the country witnessed the week-long adventure that sent a man to the moon. Families were glued to black-and-white television sets as history was made and listened to the voices at NASA describe every detail from liftoff to splashdown. Neil Armstrong proclaimed, "one small step for man," not realizing that the giant leap to follow would involve massive amounts of change and disruption in our society. That summer was the first of many when the confines of places such as Flushing, Queens, were left behind for the chance to breathe fresh air in upstate New York. It was there that the discovery of independence came with minimal parental supervision from the time school let out in June until Labor Day.

My grandparents were immigrants from Italy who made their way through Ellis Island to midtown Manhattan and eventually to Corona, Queens. They lived on 111th Street, two blocks from the elevated number seven train that would take you to Times Square in about 40 minutes. They were also within walking distance of Flushing Meadows Park, the site of the 1964 World's Fair and the same location as the 1939 World's Fair, which was dismantled so that the materials could be repurposed for use during World War II. The centerpiece of the 1964 World's Fair exhibits was the Hall of Science. My fascination with science, exploration, and imagination began during the long walks taken with my grandmother through Flushing Meadows. Computer technology was being touted by IBM, one of the lead sponsors. Mainframe computers could process information for use by large companies. Speed and efficiency were the primary drivers. Young people were learning about different worlds, about exploring the future, and about dealing with life, one crisis at a time.

By the time of the Apollo 11 mission, the sisters of Saint Joseph at Mary's Nativity School were teaching all the children within a 20-block radius. There was a bonding experience between parents in our close-knit community and relatives who worked at IBM and Grumman Aerospace, which manufactured much of the equipment that NASA used. The late fall of 1969 delivered to the neighborhood children an amazing experience: the Miracle Mets would pull off one of the greatest upsets in sports history by defeating the Baltimore Orioles in five games to win the World Series. Little did we know that nine years later almost every sixth grader would be hired as a vendor at Shea Stadium, home to the Mets and across the street from Flushing Meadows Park. Because all World Series games were played during the day, one of the nuns uncharacteristically wheeled televisions into each classroom so students could watch the live broadcast—provided, of course, that the noise level was kept to a minimum. One teacher, Mrs. Yost, was the sister of the third-base coach for the Mets, Eddie Yost. In fact, most players lived in the neighborhood in modest homes that were within walking distance to the ballpark.

Across the street from the Saint Mary's schoolyard were a series of Dutch colonial homes, each with its own driveway barely wide enough to drive a car to the detached garage out back. During the thirty-five-minute lunch period, students could be seen gazing out the picture window that faced the school. If you were lucky enough to have a stay-at-home mom, it was just enough time for her to make you a grilled cheese sandwich and a cup of tomato soup; you waited until the last moment to dash across the street just in time for afternoon roll call.

The nuns lived in a convent adjacent to the school, effectively becoming neighbors in the community. On occasion they would be seen running errands or doing chores on their property. These were holy women called to serve God by educating young people in the local parish. They had hearts of gold and stares that would make the hair on your neck stand up. Local parents made tremendous sacrifices to send their children to Catholic schools, many working multiple jobs to afford the tuition. Good grades, hard to come by, were proof that the investment the parents made—their sacrifices of time and money—were worth it.

The commitment to get good grades was combined with the need to grow socially and spiritually. Friendships originated on the first day of class in the first grade. These young people were all children of lower middle-class families. Most were Irish and Italian who had similar family backgrounds. When school let out at three in the afternoon, they rode bicycles together through Kissena Park, played Little League, joined the Cub Scouts, and eventually made trips together to the movies, pizza places, and the Army/Navy store. Their parents were the den mothers, coaches, and chaperones of the school trips. It took a village to raise them, so they all ended up with surrogate parents throughout the neighborhood.

But one thing was for sure: no matter which house you rode your bike to after school, homework had to be done immediately. In a community with so many moving parts, education was always at the center. Parents knew the opportunity for their children to have a better life would mean going to college. None of the parents in the neighborhood had a college degree. They saw the success of the astronauts, and those like them, originating in large part because of their education.

At Saint Francis Preparatory School in the fall of 1976, patriotism was at the forefront. The country's bicentennial was being celebrated with an extravagant display in New York Harbor with the Statue of Liberty as the centerpiece. Society came together as one, putting the divisiveness in the past. Less than ten years earlier, protests in the streets vehemently opposed the nation's participation in the Vietnam War. Clearly it took something extraordinary to bring everyone together as one. What was learned during that time of crisis is that a common purpose would cast away the fears and propel us into a new orbit.

Education for me was more than just an experience; it was a passion. The journey that would lead to the Bronx, studying at Fordham University, would result in not one but three degrees: bachelor's, master's, and doctorate. Navigating the academic arena would include teaching, administrative functions, and most important, fund-raising. Building relationships with key stakeholders would open doors never before conceivable. The college presidency, while a dream realized, has evolved significantly since I first was appointed thirteen years ago.

As a newly recruited college president charged to lead Endicott College on the north shore of Boston in 2019, I never could have imagined how drastically things would change during my first year in office. I brought with me nine years of experience leading two other institutions through the financial hardships that the 2008 market collapse had caused. Experience, personal and professional, is a valuable commodity; no matter what the industry or challenges an organization is facing, it allows one to draw on the past to help navigate to the future. The job of a college president is not so much to oversee the operations of today but, rather, provide the vision for the institution in the years ahead.

The week of March 9, 2020, was the beginning of the end for the way colleges traditionally operated. Our team was on the west coast of Florida getting ready for the Saint Patrick's Day Parade in Naples, which was to take place on Saturday, March 14. We had hosted several dinners earlier in the week as news of the coronavirus pandemic began to spread in the northeast. The mood in Florida was surprisingly calm as people moved around freely without much fear of the virus spreading. One news story was about a man who tested positive after a JetBlue flight from New York to West Palm Beach. But not until Thursday, March 12, when Disney World announced it was shutting its doors, that panic began to settle around us. We immediately booked flights for Friday morning, shopped for masks and hand wipes, and eventually made our way to Fort Myers to begin our journey home.

The flight to Boston was the most nerve-racking experience of my life. Fear of the unknown caused everyone to act cautiously and with great trepidation. We each asked ourselves if the person next to us could be carrying this deadly disease. This was a case of not being able to identify the enemy, much like those battles fought in the jungles of Vietnam. It was survival of the fittest with a bit of luck. The randomness of the seat assignments, the order of the boarding process, the demeanor of fellow passengers all contributed to the angst within each of us. When the plane finally landed three hours later, we grabbed our bags and raced through the terminal to find our car so we could return home. Yet even home had its share of unknowns.

College presidents are tasked with making decisions on an hourly basis. As one whose discernment process is data driven, the onset of the pandemic left me with little to no relatable information or a playbook to follow. However, one thing was crystal clear: any path forward would require some level of risk, which had to be balanced by the effort to keep everyone safe and healthy. Testing, masks, vaccines, large gatherings—the pandemic taught the world to mitigate high amounts of risk. As we transition into the endemic phase of COVID-19, colleges and universities must now move from that risk-averse mind-set to embrace the necessary risks that will carry them into the future.

Although only nine months into my tenure as Endicott College's new president, I had occupied the corner office at other institutions for nearly a decade. Using a unique business model and student-first mentality, Endicott emerged as a rare pandemic success story as we not only navigated the pandemic, but we found ourselves in a stronger position than ever before.

DIVERSIFY YOUR "PORTFOLIO"

To prepare for the next crisis, higher education institutions must prioritize financial nimbleness. Endicott College was fortunate in that auxiliary revenue from the unique business model—it operates an on-site restaurant; two award-winning wedding venues, a 99-room hotel, and a conference center—helped significantly offset early pandemic expenses, including refunding $9.2 million in room and board to software licensing for remote learning.

Most campuses do not offer a booming wedding business, but institutions had to begin adapting operations, buildings, and thinking outside the box to identify and generate alternative revenue sources. Because much of Endicott's auxiliary revenue comes from the summer months (weddings, travel, etc.)—a historically safe season in the pandemic—that was a consideration when reimagining ways an institution makes money. The goal became a model that was both sustainable and resilient rather than being solely reliant upon tuition revenue.

CREATE A CULTURE OF SAFETY

Pandemic decision making at Endicott was bolstered by savvy financial planning but defined by one question: Are we doing our best to serve our students? After shifting to a fully remote classroom for the spring semester 2020, students were back on campus to start the new academic year because we believed that it was in their best interest. Endicott's educational model relied on experiential learning and internships, and our tight-knit campus is filled with student organizations and events that are integral in shaping the next generation of global leaders. But to get students back to learning and living on campus, we had to first create a culture of safety—from testing to investing in mental health resources.

That meant establishing on-site testing sites staffed with redeployed employees whose work was not possible (coaches, athletic trainers, etc.) and mandating a zero-tolerance testing policy—100% compliance was required to be safe and instill confidence in the community. We also de-densified residence halls, leveraging our own conference center and hotel to house students, as well as those in quarantine or isolation. Hopefully, we never have to return to this mode, but institutions should have a contingency plan for worst-case scenarios and the infrastructure to pivot quickly.

Bringing students back to in-person living, learning, and socializing also helped restore normalcy and boost overall mental health of everyone on campus, which remains a top priority. During the pandemic, we established a new wellness center and switched health-care providers to improve the continuum of care on campus and better address ongoing pandemic challenges through a campus-based clinic that can treat students on-site.

Mental health concerns are not just restricted to the pandemic—they are here to stay. Just think: a majority of incoming first-year students spent half of their high-school experience behind a computer screen. Many lost parents, grandparents, and friends to the COVID-19 virus. Many students' families faced a financial crisis. There is no denying that young people missed out on critical and formative experiences and that the pandemic exacerbated feelings of loneliness and desperation. Institutions must continue to do more for student mental health and should expect to deal with the pandemic-related wellness concerns for many years to come.

HIGH-RISK DECISIONS ARE SOMETIMES REWARDED

In 2020, we offset nearly $8 million in decreased cost-of-attendance revenue with ancillary revenue, never needing to touch Endicott's endowment principal. In fact, we made our annual contribution to the endowment and still ended the year on a $15-million operating margin. In addition, while we were refunding room and board in Spring 2020, we heard from some families who said they did not need a refund, so we created the Wings Fund, which allowed families who were able to support those who were facing personal financial crises. Much like the One Fund that assisted families after the Boston Marathon bombing, the Wings Fund allowed students facing financial hardship to continue their studies due to the generosity of members of the Endicott community.

After mitigating the impact of a revenue downturn, we received government relief money that we did not anticipate—dollars we used to reinvest in the college to secure its future. Employees never missed a paycheck, received full benefits including matches to their retirement fund, and we even honored the faculty contract with an annual cost-of-living increase. Rewarding employees was also a priority, so we deployed a one-time bonus for everyone at the end of the calendar year.

When campus tours began in the fall of 2020, prospective students and their parents spoke with faculty, saw classrooms in action, ate in the dining hall, and visited classrooms, labs, and residence hall rooms. Instead of pointing to buildings or being given a self-guided tour map, our community became active members of the admissions team. Last year, we enrolled the second-largest class in the history of Endicott College, and today we are selecting from a record number of highly qualified applicants. Another unexpected outcome? Endicott's first-year retention rate increased by five percentage points to 88%.

The future of higher education is complicated and, much like the pandemic, riddled with unknowns. Although some seek to find absolutes on either end of the spectrum that will eliminate COVID-19 from the landscape, we chose to find room in the middle to mitigate risk, keep our community safe, and provide a student experience that not only transfers knowledge but allows our students to grow academically, socially, spiritually, and athletically. One thing is certain: COVID-19 has permanently altered the higher education landscape, and it is time for institutions to not only embrace risk but rewrite their crisis management playbooks altogether.

Leading in a time of crisis involves a series of decisions that must be made, often without precedence. Life experiences supply the rationale for the decision-making process to manifest, whether that be in space exploration or a once-in-a-century pandemic.

Chapter 8

Teacher Education Accreditation
Reflections on the Kennedy-Johnson Legacy of Institutional Reform

James G. Cibulka

My generation of pre-baby boomers was born at the end of World War II, grew up in the 1950s, and came of age in the 1960s. The postwar decades straddled two historic periods and national impulses. The years 1945–1960 were characterized largely by national consensus and complacency. Beneath the veneer of prosperity, however, there was what Michael Harrington (1962) referred to as "the other America" enmeshed in poverty and racial discrimination as well as a host of unaddressed national challenges.

President John F. Kennedy's election in 1960 was a symbolic break with the previous decade, signaling a new national spirit. When Kennedy proclaimed in his inaugural address that "the torch has been passed to a new generation of Americans," many of my generation understood his "New Frontier" as a summons to excellence. The youthful president implored Americans to "ask not what your country can do for you, but what you can do for your country." He inspired us to volunteer for the new Peace Corps and to pursue careers in public service. This compelling vision animated not only his presidency, but after his tragic assassination, President Lyndon Johnson's War on Poverty and, indeed, a generation of democratic reform.[1] It has since been described as a "liberal hour" in American democracy, now challenged, weakened, and even imperiled.[2]

This chapter describes how the Kennedy-Johnson legacy influenced an important chapter in my own career. Domestically, that liberal tradition focused on the use of national power to expand both excellence and equality in our nation's public-serving institutions, among them public schools and universities.³ It was an optimistic, pragmatic, rationalist vision, largely non-ideological apart from broad guiding principles and thus lent itself to different interpretations and directions.

One important focus was *institutional reform*, loosely understood as systemic changes that have the potential to redistribute benefits to underrepresented, underserved individuals and groups. This included new institutions such as community mental health centers, expansion of benefits in health care such as Medicare, unprecedented federal aid such as the landmark Elementary and Secondary Education Act (ESEA), and new voting rights and civil rights to be enforced with federal power. In their evolution, these reforms aspired to be a second New Deal. In this spirit I pursued a career as an educator with an abiding interest in how schools and universities could be reshaped to embrace more fully America's democratic ideals.

TEACHER PREPARATION AS AN INSTITUTIONAL CHALLENGE

Between 2008 and 2015, I undertook an important reform effort centered on America's system of teacher preparation. My strategy was to use the institution of national accreditation for this purpose. It is useful to begin by summarizing why teacher preparation in America needed strengthening, then and now, how the shifting politics of accountability had not achieved needed reforms, as well as why national accreditation had potential to leverage wide and sustainable reform of these preparation programs. It was, in essence, an interlocking reform strategy—stronger national accreditation, a better system of teacher preparation, and a better sourcing and supply of well-qualified teachers.

The Landscape of Teacher Preparation

The nation's system for preparing teachers has been criticized for many decades. Indeed, it hardly could be described as a coherent system at all. Historically, more than 2,000 institutions have prepared teachers (referred to hereafter as EPPs), primarily in colleges and universities. Until recently, these institutions prepared approximately 200,000 graduates annually, more than the number of positions required or filled but also producing shortages in some teaching fields.⁴ The overall quality of programs has been highly variable, some with low or nonexistent program admissions standards, weak programming, and lax exit requirements for candidates.

Although teacher preparation is a university-wide responsibility, engaging faculty in other colleges has been difficult because of the reward structure and culture of universities. Schools of education are often the lowest rung on the pecking order, sometimes a "cash cow" for the university. Unlike other professional disciplines, teacher education adopted a low-cost, liberal arts rather than clinical model (Labaree, 2004). Provosts and presidents typically pursued more prestigious priorities than the preparation of schoolteachers, and "ed school" faculty at many elite universities have placed greater priority on their research agendas than preparing teachers.

EPPs often are loosely regulated by state education departments, or in 13 states, by state professional standards boards. Differences in state regulation, as well as the state's regulatory authority and culture, have reflected whether the state is a net importer or exporter of teachers. State licensure standards often are relaxed to accommodate teaching shortages in high-needs subjects and schools. Unlike nearly any other profession, candidates can become teachers through "alternative routes," in some cases while teaching without direct oversight by a licensed teacher. The rationale for such exceptions typically has been to reduce shortages or improve overall teacher quality, a worthwhile goal to be sure.

Indeed, the quality of the teaching force has declined over many decades as more career opportunities opened for women (Wilson & Kelley, 2022). The percentage of teachers of color has continued to lag behind the growing diversity of the nation's student body, reflecting the low prestige of teaching as a career, inadequate salaries, lack of recruitment policies by many EPPs,[5] and no doubt, a legacy of racism in higher education.

Reform of Teacher Preparation

Remedying the performance of teacher preparation nationally has also proven difficult and controversial, despite many decades of professional initiatives, foundation support, and government mandates and initiatives. There have been many analyses of these efforts and disappointments (e.g., Fraser, 2007; Labaree, 2004). Briefly stated, reformers have pursued two strategies, one focusing on strengthening the profession of teaching, including how teachers are prepared. The other has focused on efforts to hold teacher preparation institutions more accountable. Advocates for one or another strategy have come from inside the profession as well as from external actors, and although profession building or accountability have sometimes been pursued as complementary approaches to reform, they are often seen as operating in tension. As we shall see, accreditation has been caught in this debate.

Beginning with the publication of *A Nation at Risk* in 1983, the public's focus on greater accountability in public education increased. PK–12 schools experienced these political pressures directly. In that arena, the professionalized bureaucratic system that had dominated public education through much of the 20th century had given way to legal mandates, teacher unionization, and political demands for school choice from governors and various interest groups. The politics of accountability in PK–12 education was shifting to an era of "inclusion and conflict" with new demands and voices (McDermott, 2011). Among these shifts were other definitions of student equity that guaranteed not only equal access but equal student outcomes, represented by federal legislation such as the No Child Left Behind Act (NCLB) of 2001 and its reauthorization as the Every Child Succeeds Act (ESSA) of 2015.

Teacher education was not immune from these political forces. Both professionalization and accountability were pursued by reformers. On the professionalization front, high-profile reports by the Holmes Group (1986) and the Carnegie Forum on Education and the Economy (1986) called for reform of teacher education. A decade later, following the negligible progress that had ensued from these two earlier reports, there was a highly publicized national effort to replace the decentralized, loosely regulated system of teacher quality in the United States with systemic reforms. The National Commission on Teaching and America's Future (NCTAF, 1996) argued for a comprehensive approach that focused on strengthening the teaching profession through recruitment, development, and retention. Key strategies included overhauling EPPs, higher licensure standards, mentoring programs, new professional standards boards, and compensation policies that rewarded knowledge and expertise. NCTAF's creation signaled a commitment to school reform by the nation's governors, led by North Carolina's "education" Governor Jim Hunt. (Stanford professor Linda Darling-Hammond was NCTAF's executive director).

NCTAF paralleled a related effort to have teachers pursue national board certification, not unlike certification standards found in medicine and other professions. Today 130,000 teachers are nationally board certified (National Board of Professional Teaching Standards, 2022). Although this number continues to grow, it remains a small fraction of the nation's 3.2 million teachers.

NCTAF and the National Board represented the high-water mark in collaborative efforts to professionalize teacher preparation and improve teacher quality systemically. The Republican takeover of the U.S. Congress in 1994 reenergized government skeptics and education critics. In 1998 when Congress reauthorized the Higher Education Act of 1965 (HEA), it incorporated annual reporting requirements for states and institutions of higher education (IHEs) on pass rates in teacher preparation programs.[6] While teacher unions continued to champion professionalization, competing reform agendas gained momentum. Education schools, which had benefited from the institutional autonomy that colleges and universities enjoyed, were drawn into the politics of accountability already impacting PK–12 schooling.

Higher-education leaders voiced fear that the accountability policies in HEA and NCLB might extend to colleges and universities, even in noneducation fields. Meanwhile, the lamentable state of affairs in teacher preparation was described by Arthur Levine (2006), somewhat hyperbolically, as "the wild West," a landscape where anything goes. But it also presented an opportunity for national accreditation to become a stronger professional voice for reform.

THE ACCREDITATION LANDSCAPE

I chaired the Kentucky Educational Standards Board while serving as dean of education at the University of Kentucky (2002–2008). This role awakened my interest in national accreditation as a reform vehicle. Kentucky required all institutions to become nationally accredited as a condition for state approval, but it was an outlier among states. The NCTAF report had zeroed in on the weak role national accreditation played in most states because, unlike most other professions, it remained largely voluntary. When I later joined the National Council for the Accreditation of Teacher Education (NCATE) as its president in 2008, NCATE accredited 725 higher-education providers, less than half the total (and an even smaller percentage among top research universities). Virtually none of the non-higher education alternative providers were accredited, and although they were only 10% of total providers, they were a growing segment of the field.

The major trade association for higher-education teacher education providers, the American Association of College of Teacher Education (AACTE), had been an initial partnering sponsor of national accreditation dating back decades and was instrumental in NCATE's creation in 1954. Yet it had never required its members to become nationally accredited. Periodically criticisms surfaced that NCATE's standards were too numerous, vague, and its process both burdensome and duplicative of state reviews. In 1982, a committee within AACTE proposed unsuccessfully that accreditation become mandatory in exchange for reforming the NCATE process. In 1987, the organization tabled a proposal for mandatory accreditation and again in 1995 rejected a similar proposal offered by its outcoming president Richard Wisniewski; about 220 of its 720 members at the time remained unaccredited. (Another 500 were neither AACTE members nor NCATE accredited.) The proposal inspired heated debate with many long-standing objections—cost factors, the nature of the standards, the uneven quality of some of the boards of examiners, possible loss of members by AACTE, and so on (Wisniewski, 1994). Reflecting the field's deep ambivalence about accreditation, the proposal was rejected by a lopsided vote, 796–256. A significant portion of the field, particularly among private liberal-arts colleges and research universities, viewed accreditation as a brake on freedom and innovation and an unnecessary expense.[7]

Other partners in NCATE's "quadrant" governance were, second, the trade association for state commissioners/state superintendents, the Council of Chief State School Officers (CCSSO),[8] and third, the two national teacher unions, primarily the National Education Association (NEA) but also the American Federation of Teachers (NFT). The fourth quadrant consisted of a loose collection of specialized professional associations (SPAs), focused on a special curricular content area such as mathematics, grade sequence such as elementary education, or student category such as special education.

These four quadrants aspired to be seen as a broad representation of the profession, even though in practice they played different, in some ways conflicting roles. Critics charged that NCATE's financial model was flawed because it depended in part on dues from EPPs and its trade association, AACTE. In this respect, NCATE was not unique among accreditors. Self-regulation typically lacked independent funding to insulate the accreditor from accusations of bias.

NCATE had been the field's only accreditor from its inception in 1954 until 1997.[9] Although it enjoyed a strong reputation, owing in part to the leadership of my predecessor, Arthur Wise, some teacher educators found it heavy-handed, intrusive, bureaucratic, and too close to the teacher unions. A rival accreditor, the Teacher Education Accreditation Council (TEAC), had emerged in 1997 under the leadership of a former dean at the University of Delaware, Frank Murray.[10]

In contrast to NCATE, TEAC offered its members a self-study model known as an "inquiry brief," and its board consisted almost exclusively of higher-education representatives as the arbiters of quality assurance. TEAC's creation had led to sharp conflict within the profession and much confusion among stakeholders. When I arrived at NCATE, discussions had just begun to find a way to merge the two accreditors to speak with one voice and to conserve resources. Thus, it was an auspicious time to initiate reforms to teacher preparation accreditation.

Reforming NCATE Accreditation Processes

As NCATE president, I initiated reforms intended to streamline accreditation with increased rigor and relevance. I argued that programs needed to embrace a culture of continuous improvement, mirroring other high-performing organizations. This theme of continuous improvement became one of two pathways available to institutions to demonstrate that they met NCATE standards. Programs could aspire toward *excellence* rather than *adequacy* on at least one standard and receive due recognition for this achievement. A second pathway, known as transformation initiatives, was piloted to allow research universities to use their accreditation processes to test innovations and strengthen research on effective programs.[11]

Criticisms were coming from state officials and local schools that new teachers were not prepared adequately for the classroom, particularly for work in impoverished schools. I concluded that the dominant "student-teaching" model needed dramatic improvements, including the curriculum, relationships with schools, and how faculty were deployed to work in schools. To create consensus for a transition to a clinical model, I appointed a blue-ribbon panel (National Council for the Accreditation of Teacher Education, 2010), cochaired by a prominent teacher educator, Nancy Zimpher, and Colorado state superintendent of schools Dwight Jones. The panel's report was endorsed by AACTE, U.S. Secretary of Education Arne Duncan, and others. This panel report later became the basis for CAEP's clinical standard.

Unification of Accreditation: Creation of CAEP

While these NCATE reforms were underway, discussions were initiated to consider unification of NCATE and TEAC. Unification offered several potential advantages—less internal competition and conflict, more credibility with policy makers, possible mandatory accreditation for all EPPs, and a new institutional platform for systemic reforms to teacher preparation. In addition, TEAC had an additional reason to pursue unification: its business model was proving unsustainable.

In 2008, the governance boards of both organizations created a 14-member Joint Design Team to explore unification. After extensive deliberations, in 2010 NCATE and TEAC boards recommended creation of a new accreditor, the Council for the Accreditation of Educator Preparation (CAEP). Until it became fully operational in 2014, CAEP operated with an interim board, Frank Murray as chair and me as its president.[12] Murray and I reported frequently on our progress to the field, which was generally very supportive of unification.

Operationalizing CAEP

It fell to the new interim board and CAEP's president to operationalize CAEP. This proved more difficult than anyone had imagined, with many unanticipated stumbling blocks. Four tasks presented major challenges in getting the new organization up and running and creating an agreed-upon framework for CAEP implementation.

CAEP Standards and Performance Reporting

New standards were a key strategy for accomplishing CAEP's ambitious goals. The Design Team had promised "fewer, higher, and clearer" standards and common evidentiary processes. In 2012, a commission was appointed to develop standards and multiple measures of program performance. Cochairs were Camilla Benbow, dean of the college of education at Vanderbilt University; and Terry Holliday, PK–12 commissioner in Kentucky and chair of the Council of Chief State School Officers (CCSSO). CCSSO had led development of more rigorous "common core" PK–12 student standards. Many of us envisioned that CAEP could raise the bar for teacher preparation in parallel fashion. (At the time the common core standards were still popular and despite blowback from critics, were adopted by 46 states.)

CAEP's standards commission created five standards:

Standard 1: Content and Pedagogical Knowledge
Standard 2: Clinical Partnerships and Practice
Standard 3: Candidate Quality, Recruitment, and Selectivity
Standard 4: Program Impact
Standard 5: Provider Quality Assurance and Continuous Improvement

The commission solicited feedback on its draft standards. The shift in Standard 2 to a stronger clinical practice model received little pushback, perhaps because of the prior work of the NCATE Blue Ribbon Panel. Standard 3, which raised admission requirements for programs, received the most criticism. Some argued that this would reduce applicant diversity and resisted the commission's argument that programs should recruit more actively for diversity.

Another flash point was Standard 4, which held programs accountable for performance of students whom their graduates subsequently taught. This was partly philosophical and partly practical. States were only then developing longitudinal data systems to provide such information. The commission reasoned, however, that the new standard could be phased in as states developed capacity to provide programs with data on their graduates. It was careful to endorse multiple measures by which graduates' teaching competence could be demonstrated.

The commission recommended annual performance reporting to demonstrate continuous improvement. This was reflected in Standard 5. Apart from articulating general principles, the commission did not lay out specific evidence that would be required to meet this standard at an accreditation visit and annually thereafter.

At its final meeting the commission made revisions to the proposed standards but held firm overall. Leaders of the nation's two teacher unions, who served on the commission, joined in unanimous support for the new standards. NCATE, TEAC, and CAEP boards also approved the new standards without opposition. Even AACTE offered glowing comments.

The honeymoon did not last. AACTE, reflecting pressures from its member institutions, argued in early 2015 that the standards should be revised for "clarity," a move that drew sharp criticism from CAEP supporters and a negative response by the CAEP board. More concerning, however, was criticism from within the CAEP board. Murray, who had been active in the design group and worked cooperatively with the commission in developing the standards, began to raise technical and measurement questions about the standards. In addition, he began to articulate what would become a recurrent theme: that CAEP's approach to data-based decision making was too prescriptive and reminiscent of NCATE. This perspective reflected a more basic philosophical opposition to data-based decision-making principles as they had been articulated in the CAEP standards and the approach to performance reporting that the CAEP commission had endorsed. Murray had insisted on maintaining two separate accrediting commissions to protect the integrity of TEAC's inquiry-brief process. His position also was a harbinger of difficulties ahead for CAEP's promise to unify the two accreditors.

After I left CAEP in 2015,[13] the CAEP board responded to pressures by lowering the admissions standard to the 50th percentile (from the original requirement that *on average* candidates should score in the upper third on a national test) and allowed programs to demonstrate the competence of their candidates, not at admission but any time prior to a candidate's completion. Today the 50th-percentile requirement no longer appears on CAEP's website.

CAEP Governance and Funding

CAEP's 21-member board was a hybrid of NCATE and TEAC, leaning more heavily to the former. Without explicitly perpetuating NCATE's quadrants, the CAEP board mirrored the boards in many nonprofit membership organizations where paying members are given a voice.

In practice, however, this approach presented two problems. First, it ceded power for nominations to the respective member organizations, whose priority was to preserve their own voices. Recruiting innovators to the board to protect CAEP's reform mission was never seriously discussed.

Second, as a consequence various groups and individuals vied to understand and protect their role in a still inchoate organization. As new leadership for the board chair had to be recruited, the reform coalition that I had built at NCATE was lost. The new board chair was fiercely protective of the earlier

TEAC model. In retrospect it became clear, as several CAEP supporters advised me, that CAEP needed a different kind of board to advance CAEP's new organizational mission. CAEP's governance model made it financially dependent on its members, as is widely the case in accreditation. The design team had never considered a more independent funding model for the new organization, or even if that would be a possibility.

CAEP Staffing

The same logic—an adaptation to current realities—was applied to CAEP's staffing requirements. Staffing decisions were my responsibility as president. I took a relatively conservative approach for two reasons. Senior leadership familiar with NCATE and TEAC legacy processes were needed because CAEP accreditation would be phased in over seven years. Also, some staffing would need to draw on existing staff in each legacy organization to demonstrate equitable treatment and to husband finite resources.

This reality (to preserve the old while inventing the new) was an important constraint on staff performance. Short-term pressures were coming from the field and from policy makers, all eager for answers on implementation that were not immediately available. Not surprisingly, senior staff levels had continuing turnover, and as it turned out, not all appointees possessed the skill sets required. As we confronted many issues without clear answers, I favored building consensus, reflecting my background in higher education. This leadership approach, however, failed to dispel fractiousness and mutual distrust within the staff among the former NCATE and TEAC incumbents.

The Joint Design Team had avoided the word "merger" in describing the new entity it wished to create, to dispel any perception that TEAC as the smaller organization was being swallowed up by NCATE. Ironically, however, merging the two staffs was precisely what was needed for them to function effectively.

Accreditation Processes and Decisions

CAEP was built on a promise of choice among accreditation pathways. The conviction underlying this promise was that a common set of standards could lead to comparable evidentiary requirements, a necessity for CAEP to be recognized by USDOE and CHEA. However, after I left CAEP, the CAEP board was unconvinced that the two pathways offered comparable rigor and thus eliminated the inquiry brief pathway that had been a TEAC legacy process. This decision violated a core conceptual principle that had been agreed to by the Joint Design Team upon TEAC's insistence—namely, that CAEP would treat NCATE and TEAC as equals. Not surprisingly, former TEAC institutions responded by creating a new accreditor, the Association for Advancing

Quality in Educator Preparation (AAQEP) to restore a choice in accreditation. Unification was dead.

CONCLUSION: REFLECTIONS ON TEACHER PREPARATION ACCREDITATION AND INSTITUTIONAL REFORM

The "liberal hour" in American life inaugurated by the Kennedy-Johnson presidencies, despite its limitations and contradictions, motivated my generation to strengthen our nation's public-serving institutions. However, in the six decades since the Kennedy-Johnson era, the liberal hour has dissipated (Boyle, 2021; Andersen, 2020) and along with it the optimistic liberal consensus that animated these reforms. CAEP offers a case study of the complexities, if not pitfalls, surrounding efforts to undertake significant reforms in America's public-serving institutions.

This breakdown of consensus about the liberal tradition of institutional reform has been driven by many factors. Compared with the last major period of national institutional reforms initiated in the 1960s and 1970s, much of the public now distrusts our public-serving institutions, including government itself. This has been fueled by conservative attacks on governmental legitimacy and performance dating back to Goldwater, Watergate, and subsequent societal disruptions such as COVID-19 (Fried & Harris, 2021). Right-wing populist attacks on experts and professional "elites" have also played a role in eroding public trust in our democratic institutions, civil society, and their leaders (Nichols, 2017).

Competing academic perspectives on institutional reform are also a by-product of the diverse academic perspectives on institutional reform that have emerged since the 1960s. There is no longer an accepted narrative about how to define institutional reform, how to achieve it, or how to measure it. As a result, any effort to interpret CAEP as a success or failure of institutional reform is subject to rival interpretations. To illustrate this, I explore briefly several competing interpretations that can be applied to analyze CAEP.[14]

A PLURALIST PERSPECTIVE ON CAEP: AN EXERCISE IN COMPROMISE

Political pluralism offers one valuable, if ultimately inadequate, perspective on CAEP. Interest-group theorists (e.g., Dahl, 1967; Truman, 1951) argue that voluntary groups mobilize competitively in public-serving institutions to secure benefits. In the political system of checks and balances designed by our founders, no single group consistently mobilizes or wins, coalitions shift with issues and interests, and conflict is mediated by compromises. All parties share incremental gains over time. Pursuit of the public interest is an ongoing process of give-and-take rather than a finite outcome.

From this pluralist perspective, CAEP's performance can be understood as the outcome of political compromises. NCATE and TEAC came together to secure benefits they could not obtain individually but were in their mutual self-interest. Rigorous CAEP standards were created by a broad coalition of interests. These standards were later revised by the CAEP board under pressure from interest groups, primarily voices within the profession. The same mutual accommodations characterized CAEP's governance, staffing, and other dimensions. No group got entirely what it wanted, but compromises preserved some reforms. Pluralism is an exercise in optimism; over the long term the give-and-take of compromise produces the best outcomes possible.

As one might expect, CAEP's leadership expressed optimistic assumptions; CAEP president Christopher Koch observed that "CAEP can absolutely get there," claiming that the organization was listening and had been responsive (Sawchuck, 2016).

This pluralist interpretation suffers from two limitations. One is its exclusive focus on process. It lacks any external criterion against which to evaluate CAEP's performance. Accordingly, whether CAEP has moved the field of educator preparation accreditation forward is outside the scope of pluralist theory. A second much-criticized limitation of pluralist theory is that it assumes a parity of power among stakeholders producing if not optimal, at least satisfactory outcomes. The theoretical perspectives discussed next offer additional insights on CAEP that move beyond pluralist interpretations.

A POLICY-OUTCOMES PERSPECTIVE ON CAEP

One perspective reflects the policy-studies scholarship that emerged in the 1970s. This perspective evaluates would-be reforms such as CAEP on whether it has produced the outcomes it originally promised its stakeholders, or at least whether it has progressed toward meeting its original goals.[15] From a policy-outcomes perspective, we can ask about CAEP's policy achievements after its first seven years of implementation.

One of its promises was to unify the profession. However, as previously discussed, a new accreditor, AAQEP, emerged to compete with CAEP after it eliminated a choice of pathways. This effectively reinstates the earlier division of accreditation approaches between NCATE and TEAC.

Another CAEP aspiration was to increase the appeal of accreditation to states and EPPs. Yet today the two accreditors, like their predecessors, accredit roughly 47% of the nation's 1,455 traditional and alternative higher-education EPPs. CAEP has succeeded in accrediting only a small number of the nation's 224 alternative non-IHE programs despite the growing proportion of providers from this sector.[16] CAEP's most recent reported membership is 627 (Council for the Accreditation of Educator Preparation, 2021) while AAQEP (Association for Advancing Quality in Educator Preparation, 2022) reports 61 (and some of these are different programs at the same institution).[17]

CAEP also promised to raise the bar in educator preparation. Therefore, one key measure of CAEP's performance would be how often it has denied or revoked accreditation to programs failing to meet its standards. Table 8.1 enumerates the decisions made in the most recent reporting period, Fall and Spring 2021, as well as the cumulative total of CAEP decisions since 2014.[18]

By way of information, CAEP's accreditation council(s) have five possible accreditation decision outcomes: accreditation, accreditation with stipulation (one or more systemic concerns or serious deficiencies); accreditation with areas for improvement (AFIs) that constitute less serious deficiencies; accreditation on probation (one standard is not met); denial or revocation (more than one standard is not met). As table 8.1 indicates, most decisions led to accreditation with no stipulations or probation. Only 11% between 2014 and 2021 were placed on probation, 10.4% were given stipulations, and only one had accreditation revoked or denied. Decisions for the most recent year reported (2021) mirrored this historic pattern of largely positive outcomes for providers seeking CAEP accreditation.[19] Based on these data, CAEP has not delivered on its promise to bring greater rigor to accreditation. In sum, an outcome perspective reveals a discernible gap between CAEP's original goals and its subsequent performance as an organization of change.

Table 8.1. CAEP Accreditation Decisions

Time Frame	Decision Outcome			
	Accreditation	Accreditation on Probation	Accreditation with Stipulations	Revocation or Denial of Accreditation
All Decisions 2014–2021	413	46 (11%)	43 (10.4%)	1 (.002%)
2021 Decisions Only	161*	12 (7.5%)	3 (0.9%)	0

Note: * Reflects total number of decisions on initial and advanced programs (reported only for 2021.) Percentages are calculated from raw numbers as reported in CAEP Annual Report (2021).

CAEP AS A POWER IMBALANCE: TWO COMPETING VIEWS

A third theoretical perspective explains CAEP's performance problems as a reflection of a power imbalance among stakeholders, contrary to pluralist theory. In this model the distribution of power among stakeholders is skewed to favor some interests over others. The theoretical underpinning for this perspective is that accreditation, like American democracy, depends on "countervailing powers" and "participatory democracy" to prevent dominance favoring one set of political or institutional interests.[20]

But a power imbalance model lends itself to different interpretations as to who benefits or is harmed. These differing interpretations are discussed next.

Disempowered Professionals

Some professional voices in teacher preparation argue that accountability policies in accreditation have disempowered professionals. Cochran-Smith et al. (2018) blame CAEP's creation on "neoliberal" elites. These CAEP critics believe that professionals should be the key stakeholder in accreditation and wish to guard professional autonomy. Their rationale is that autonomy is a necessary precondition for EPPs to generate knowledge to improve their local programs. However, in asserting professional control, these critics are not necessarily in agreement as to how limited an accreditor's role should be. For example, although Wojcikiewicz and Patrick (2022) agree with critics that CAEP's agenda diminishes professionalization, they recommend using licensure standards to judge candidates and programs.[21]

The debate over professional self-regulation and how to balance professional authority with the public interest is an old one and not limited to education. A full discussion is beyond the scope of this chapter. However, it should be noted that other professions support mandatory accreditation as an indispensable component of a strong profession. Unfortunately, education has been unable to achieve a fundamental precondition on which strong accreditation rests—namely, a professional consensus on the need to regulate the quality of programs. This professional void has deep historical roots, contrasting education with many other professions (Mehta, 2013).

Regulatory Capture

A different interpretation of the power imbalance model is that CAEP suffers from regulatory capture by the profession itself. The capture model suggests that professional interests have usurped control over national accreditation.

In the classic case of traditional regulatory theory (e.g., public utilities producing gas or electricity), government regulation should act as a countervailing power to protect the public interest. However, the regulated parties can "capture" the process to their advantage (Carpenter & Moss, 2014). This capture can also occur in education, whether the regulators are accreditors or state governments.[22]

Capture can take different forms. For example, "corrosive capture" occurs when an accreditor depends financially on the EPPs it regulates, creating a disincentive to employ its regulatory authority appropriately. "Cultural capture" occurs when EPPs shape information available to state regulators.[23] Regulators and EPPs share similar professional training and socialization, which can create regulator bias favoring EPPs.

Considerable evidence supports the capture model when applied to teacher prep accreditation, long preceding CAEP. NCATE rarely denied accreditation to an EPP. Despite this leniency, AACTE did not require its members to be accredited, and only a few of CCSSO's member states mandated national accreditation. Consequently, more than half of the nation's EPPs remained unaccredited. Teacher unions were largely concerned about assuring their voice in any effort to professionalize the field, including accreditation. They recognized that they would benefit from cultivating a professional image instead of the more mundane concerns about salaries, benefits, and working conditions normally associated with labor unions. For their part, the specialty organizations (SPAs) joined national accreditation primarily to expand their own professional reach and were only minimally concerned about rigor elsewhere in CAEP outside their specific program specialties.

Although CAEP had the potential to disrupt this legacy that had bedeviled teacher preparation, not surprisingly its key stakeholders found reasons to resist a stronger accreditation system. Many AACTE members recognized immediately that they might have difficulty passing the new CAEP standards and pressured AACTE to resist them. Teacher unions strengthened their alliance with AACTE because they were displeased with CAEP's intent to evaluate subsequent classroom performance of EPP graduates. This standard conflicted with their efforts to preserve the status quo in teacher evaluation systems.

CCSSO was a potential counterforce to this backpedaling by AACTE and the unions. Because of its long-standing dissatisfaction with the products of education schools. Its leadership had played a strong role in creating rigorous CAEP standards and had pushed back against union efforts on the commission to water down program impact requirements (Standard 4). Nonetheless, CCSSO remained largely passive when CAEP later faced challenges from other stakeholders. At this time, CCSSO was facing mounting challenges to its leadership from a growing number of state commissioners who, among other things, were antagonistic to teacher unions and questioned the value and cost of national accreditation.[24] CCSSO also became embroiled in a controversy over federal/national overreach concerning the common core standards that it helped develop. In view of these internal divisions and challenges, CCSSO's voice defending CAEP against AACTE's broadsides was necessarily muted.

The remaining group of stakeholders, the SPAs, failed to coalesce to defend CAEP's new approach to quality assurance. This reflected their relatively autonomous and diminishing role in CAEP compared with NCATE. CAEP had been unable to resolve the long-standing tension within accreditation over how to evaluate subject matter coverage (e.g., math, science, etc.) in preparation programs. To diminish EPPs' criticism of SPAs, CAEP initiated its own review process that SPAs saw as less rigorous. Although most SPAs have remained inside CAEP, are concerns continue about the costs of maintaining their review processes within CAEP. In 2022 one SPA, the International Society for Technology in Education (ISTE), withdrew from CAEP altogether to conduct its own review process (Klein, 2022). Whether this is a precursor of other SPA withdrawals is unclear.

In sum, for a brief time the stakeholders responsible for teaching one of the weakest and least-respected professions came together to build a new accreditation enterprise committed to accountability and rigor. Ironically, however, CAEP exposed the long-standing partisan interests that impede strong quality assurance in teacher preparation. The lack of countervailing power and participatory democracy within CAEP's governance and accreditation processes instantiated the voice of producers (EPPs, states, unions, and SPAs). The needs and interests of school districts, PK–12 students, candidates, and the public constituencies that would benefit from a stronger teaching force and a strong, effective CAEP had no direct voice in CAEP's governance. Given this uneven distribution of institutional power, regulatory capture provides the most compelling explanation for why CAEP's performance has not measured up to the stated aspirations. CAEP's performance is largely a reflection of what the governing stakeholders agreed to expect from CAEP.

Reformers in the Kennedy-Johnson era were not naive about the challenges they faced. They recognized that institution building and reform would require additional public investments, that vested interests—among them from professionals—would likely attempt to block or weaken reform, and that new political coalitions would have to be built to empower the poor, racial minorities, consumers, and other stakeholders. Nonetheless, they were optimistic that lasting reform could prevail despite short-term challenges, particularly if undertaken nationally to counter vested state and local interests. Undergirding this optimism was a shared faith, across the political spectrum and citizenry, in the American political tradition of pluralism, pragmatism, compromise, and progress.

To a remarkable degree, albeit on a narrower scale, CAEP's challenges illustrate a fundamental crisis confronting our nation: how to restore effectiveness and support for our public-serving institutions. Although there is no consensus on how this renewal can be accomplished, a strategy of indifference or inaction would be a serious, potentially fatal, mistake.

The circumstances of America in the Kennedy-Johnson era were very different from our own, but the power of generational change is equally relevant today. John Kennedy's inaugural address might serve as a starting point for today's leaders. Kennedy reached out to "a new generation of Americans" to address the relationship between duty and power, calling on the nation to combat "the common enemies of man: tyranny, poverty, disease, and war itself" and entreating each American to commit ourselves personally to the betterment of our country.

What my generation failed to accomplish, often despite our best efforts, across the changing landscape of American life since the 1960s must be taken up by a new generation of Americans. Evidence is encouraging that America's youth recognize the formidable challenges facing our nation and planet, and that they are impatient to address those imperatives. Nothing less than a renewed faith in our democracy and the preservation of our core democratic values is at stake.

NOTES

1. Because the Johnson presidency in a sense sought to complete the agenda of Kennedy's presidency, I have chosen to describe them in this essay as one historic period and legacy.

2. The "liberal hour" is taken from the excellent biography of Ted Kennedy by Gabler (2020).

3. In this chapter I treat government institutions such as public schools and nonprofit institutions such as the many colleges and universities, as well as most accreditors, similarly. They can be distinguished from for-profit institutions in critical respects—their missions, legal requirements, regulatory environments, and governance. Although governments and nonprofit organizations are not identical, I refer to them as "public regarding" institutions.

4. In recent years enrollments in colleges of education and the number of annual graduates has declined, creating more widespread teaching shortages beyond traditional shortage fields and regions (Wilson & Kelley, 2022).

5. In universities with undergraduate teacher education majors, EPPs typically draw their candidates from the existing baccalaureate classes.

6. Many programs found a loophole, however, by manipulating how they reported a candidate's pass rate, achieving a 100% score. Title II also authorized competitive grants to improve the quality of teacher-preparation programs.

7. The debate continued throughout my tenure as NCATE president and later as CAEP's founding president. CAEP resurfaced the decades-old debate about whether accreditation's primary role should be profession-defined accountability to meet rigorous standards or self-improvement. Controversy has persisted. Most recently in 2018 AACTE, facing continuing resistance to CAEP among its membership, found it necessary to convene a national conference on accreditation, which concluded by reaffirming its commitment to a unified national professional accreditation system, but in a seeming contradiction and nod to political reality, it acknowledged the right of "each state and institution to determine the appropriate national or state processes it deems suitable" (AACTE, 2018). It is important to note that this debate over how to define the profession's aims, its membership, and its relationship to state authority reaches beyond accreditation. For example, criticisms of NCTAF's approach to professionalization paralleled those about accreditation (Fraser, 2007). Such debates help explain AACTE's uneasy relationship to NCATE and CAEP. Other perennial sources of tension included AACTE's claim that its dues to NCATE and later CAEP were excessive, as well as other disagreements over the two organizations' overlapping responsibilities.

8. Individual states participated in NCATE's state partnership program, paid dues, and gained an indirect voice in governance through CCSSO's seats on the NCATE board.

9. NCATE accredited education units preparing education professionals in PK–12 schools serving in a variety of roles. My focus here, for reasons of space alone, is on the largest category, teacher-preparation programs.

10. TEAC represented a small but growing addition to the total number of accredited IHEs, 190 in 2012. It should be noted that because the U.S. Department of Education double counts some IHEs, those that have both a traditional and alternative program, the total number of U.S. providers can only be estimated.

11. Research on effective programs for preparing teachers was notoriously weak, and many EPP faculty at research universities had complained that accreditation detracted from their research agendas.

12. NCATE and TEAC were dissolved as operational entities. They remained in place legally until all institutions were accredited by CAEP.

13. I left CAEP voluntarily in May 2015.

14. Space precludes a comprehensive treatment of analytical frameworks that might be applied to understand CAEP. The frameworks discussed here are drawn from political science and policy research. These frameworks provide a potential "good fit" because of the ambiguous goals, means, and outcomes in public-serving organizations such as CAEP.

15. Implementation studies and policy evaluation research emerged in the 1970s, partly in response to disappointing results of many 1960s reforms (Allison, 1971; Lasswell, 1971; Pressman & Wildavsky, 1973). Although implementation research focuses on post-adoption processes that might undermine reforms, policy evaluation

research examines outcomes, often independent of the processes that produced them. In PK–12 education policy, the shift toward measuring school performance with student outcomes, a development that James Coleman launched in 1966, increased the saliency of outcome research.

16. The alternative non-IHE programs grew 11% between 2012–2013 and 2018–2019 (U.S. Department of Education, 2022).

17. Anecdotal evidence indicates that CAEP continues to lose members each year, some of whom may gravitate to AAQEP, but may result in a net loss of members among the two the accreditors.

18. CAEP's annual report does not enumerate accreditations with areas for improvement (AFIs), so these cannot be reported.

19. There are, of course, additional ways to evaluate CAEP's policy outcomes. For example, CAEP standards also focused on improving the qualifications and diversity of America's teaching force.

20. John Kenneth Galbraith (1993), a leading economist and prominent intellectual in the Kennedy administration, articulated the concept of "countervailing power" to address the changing circumstances of American capitalism in the post–World War II period. He argued that where markets do not create countervailing powers, the government must intervene to reduce monopoly power. A parallel theme in the Kennedy-Johnson years was participatory democracy, an effort to expand voices in the governance of public-regarding institutions with "maximum feasible participation" in the War of Poverty, community mental health programs, and other reform initiatives. Participatory democracy has been a continuous strand in democratic theory dating back to the Athenians, with many current formulations (Bherer, Dufour, & Montambeault, 2016). Both countervailing power and participatory democracy seek to prevent a dominance in policy making by a narrow set of interests.

21. It is unclear how this would differ from CAEP. Wojcikiewicz and Patrick (2022) advocate a greater emphasis on continuous improvement but overlook that CAEP Standard 5 requires EPPs to develop a quality assurance system focused on use of data and continuous improvement processes. See http://www.caepnet.org/standards/archive-standards/2013-itp/standard-5. They also argue for program impact measures that are in CAEP Standard 4. See https://caepnet.org/standards/2022-itp/standard-4.

22. The legacy of weak state regulation of teacher preparation lends considerable support to a capture model. State education departments have suffered from chronic weaknesses, despite federal aid to strengthen their capacity and increased expectations for their performance (Anagnostopoulos, Rutledge, & Bali, 2013; Center on Education Policy, 2012.) Early in their development "state education bureaucracies became dominated by professional interests" (Timar, 1997, p. 241, as cited in McDermott, 2011, p. 37). Despite federal requirements that ask states to designate and close "low-performing" teacher-preparation programs, few have done so (Crowe, 2011; U.S. Government Accountability Office, 2015). According to the U.S. Department of Education (2022, p. 24, supplemental table S2.5), as of 2018–2019, states had designated only 72 teacher preparation providers out of 2,178 as having at least one at-risk or low-performing program, and these were concentrated in only three states. The remaining 47 states designated no low-performing programs.

23. Principal-agent theory in behavioral economics and other academic disciplines point to this asymmetrical information as a power imbalance. Public bureaucracies including regulatory agencies such as state education agencies offer many examples of the principal-agent problem. For a summary and critique, see Waterman & Meier, 1998. Chubb and Moe (1990) offer the classic analysis applied to PK–12 public education.

REFERENCES

AACTE. (2018, January 30). *AACTE board reaffirms the importance of national accreditation for educator preparation.* https://aacte.org/2018/01/aacte-board-reaffirms-importance-of-national-accreditation-for-educator-preparation/

Allison, G. (1971). *Essence of decision: Explaining the Cuban missile crisis.* Boston: Little, Brown.

Anagnostopoulos, D., Rutledge, S., and Bali, V. (2013). State education agencies, information systems, and the expansion of state power in the era of test-based accountability. *Education Policy, 27*(2), 217–247.

Andersen, K. (2020). *Evil geniuses: The unmaking of America: A recent history.* New York: Penguin Random House.

Association for Advancing Quality in Educator Preparation. (2022). *Accredited programs.* https://aaqep.org/accredited-programs

Bherer, L., Dufour, P. & Montambeault, F. (2016). The participatory democracy turn: An introduction. *Journal of Civil Society, 12*(3), 225–230. DOI: 10.1080/17448689.2016.1216383

Boyle, K. (2021). *The shattering: America in the 1960s.* New York: Norton.

Carnegie Forum on Education and the Economy (1986). *A nation prepared: Teachers for the 21st century: The report of the Task Force on Teaching as a Profession.* New York: Author.

Carpenter, D., and Moss, D. A. (Eds.). (2014). *Preventing regulatory capture: Special interest influence and how to limit it.* New York: Cambridge University Press.

Center on Education Policy. (2012). *State education agency funding and staffing in the education reform era.* George Washington University, Center on Education Policy. https://files.eric.ed.gov/fulltext/ED529269.pdf

Chubb, J. E., and Moe, T. M. (1990). *Politics, markets, and America's schools.* Washington, DC: Brookings Institution Press.

Cochran-Smith, M., Carney, M. C., Keefe, E. S., Burton, S., Chang, W., Fernandez, M. B., . . . Baker, M. (2018). *Reclaiming accountability in teacher education.* New York: Teachers College Press.

Council for the Accreditation of Educator Preparation. (2021). *Annual report.* https://caepnet.org/~/media/Files/caep/governance/caep-annualreport2021.pdf?la=en

Crowe, E. (2011). *Getting better at teacher preparation and state accountability: Strategies, innovations, and challenges under the federal Race to the Top program.* https://files.eric.ed.gov/fulltext/ED535643.pdf

Dahl, R. (1967). *Pluralistic democracy in the United States: Conflict and consent.* Chicago: Rand-MacNally.

Fraser, J. W. (2007). *Preparing America's teachers: A history.* New York: Teachers College Press.

Fried, A., and Harris, D. B. (2021). *At war with government: How conservatives weaponized distrust from Goldwater to Trump.* New York: Columbia University Press.

Gabler, N. (2020). *Catching the wind: Ted Kennedy and the liberal hour 1932–1975.* New York: Random House.

Galbraith, J. K. (1993). *American capitalism: The concept of countervailing power.* New York: Routledge.

Harrington, M. D. (1962). *The other America: Poverty in the United States.* Baltimore, MD: Penguin.

Holmes Group. (1986). *Tomorrow's teachers: A report of the Holmes Group.* East Lansing, MI.

Klein, A. (2022, September 22). Education professional development superpower? ISTE and ASCD set to merge. *Education Week.* https://www.edweek.org/leadership/education-professional-development-superpower-iste-and-ascd-set-to-merge/2022/09?s_kwcid=AL!6416!3!602270476281!!!g!!&utm_source=goog&utm_medium=cpc&utm_campaign=ew+dynamic+recent&ccid=dynamic+ads+recent+articles&ccag=recent+articles+dynamic&cckw=&cccv=dynamic+ad&gclid=CjwKCAiAzKqdBhAnEiwAePEjknzT-wyxHV6ZyRbp6ZD3kqKmt4jPIRaS0rN5nrMUQE8-QfEKdiEEmRoCtk4QAvD_BwE

Labaree, D. F. (2004). *The trouble with ed schools.* New Haven, CT: Yale University Press.

Lasswell, H. D. (1971). *A preview of policy sciences.* New York: American Elsevier.

Levine, A. (2006). *Educating school teachers.* Princeton, NJ. http://edschools.org/pdf/Educating_Teachers_Report.pdf

McDermott, K. A. (2011). *High-stakes reform: The politics of educational accountability.* Washington, DC: Georgetown University Press.

Mehta, J. (2013). *The allure of order: High hopes, dashed expectations, and the troubled quest to remake American schooling.* New York: Oxford University Press.

National Board of Professional Teaching Standards. (2022). *More than 2,000 teachers earn National Board certification; 130,000 now teach to the profession's highest standards.* https://www.nbpts.org/newsroom/more-than-2000-teachers-earn-national-board-certification-130000-now-teach-to-the-professions-highest-standards/

National Commission on Teaching and America's Future. (1996). *What matters most: Teaching for America's future.* Washington, DC: Author.

National Council for the Accreditation of Teacher Education. (2010). Transforming teacher education through clinical practice: A national strategy to prepare effective teachers. Report of the Blue Ribbon Panel on Clinical Preparation and Partnerships. http://caepnet.org/~/media/Files/caep/accreditation-resources/blue-ribbon-panel.pdf

Nichols, T. (2017). *The death of expertise: The campaign against established knowledge and why it matters.* New York: Oxford University Press.

Pressman, J. L., and Wildavsky, A. (1973). *Implementation: How great expectations in Washington are dashed in Oakland.* Berkeley: University of California Press.

Sawchuck, S. (2016, August 23). Teacher-prep accreditation group seeks to regain traction. *Education Week.* https://www.edweek.org/teaching-learning/teacher-prep-accreditation-group-seeks-to-regain-traction/2016/08

Timar, T. (1997). The institutional role of state education departments: A historical perspective. *American Journal of Education, 105* (May), 231–260.

Truman, D. B. (1951). *The governmental process: Political interests and public opinion.* New York: Knopf.

U.S. Department of Education (2022). *Preparing and credentialing the nation's teachers: The Secretary's report on the teacher workforce.* https://title2.ed.gov/Public/OPE%20Annual%20Report.pdf

U.S. Government Accountability Office. (2015, July). *Teacher preparation programs: Education should ensure states identify low performing, programs and improve information sharing* (Report No. GAO-15–598). House of Representatives, Committee on Education and the Workforce, Subcommittee on Health, Employment, Labor, and Pensions. https://www.gao.gov/assets/680/671603.pdf

Vilky, E. (2022). *State partnership agreements.* http://caepnet.org/about/news-room/state-partnership-agreements

Waterman, R.W., and Meier, K. J. (1998). Principal-agent models: An expansion? *Journal of Public Administration and Theory, 8*(2), 173–202.

Wilson, S. M., & Kelley, S. L. (2022). *Landscape of teacher preparation programs and teacher candidates.* National Academy of Education Committee on Evaluating and Improving Teacher Preparation Programs. Washington, DC: National Academy of Education.

Wisniewski, R. (1994, November–December) Accreditation and leadership. *Journal of Teacher Education, 45*(5). https://journals.sagepub.com/doi/abs/10.1177/0022487194045005002

Wojcikiewicz, S. K., & Patrick, S. K. (2022). *The evolution of accreditation as professional quality assurance in teacher preparation.* National Academy of Education Committee on Evaluating and Improving Teacher Preparation Programs. Washington, DC: National Academy of Education.

Chapter 9

Standing on Their Shoulders

Contextual Change to Our Education System in the 21st Century

Paige Hendricks

The field of education is in a continual state of evolution. Changes to the demographics, ability levels of students, and to broader societal dynamics require educators to regularly update curricular approaches and instructional strategies. Periodically, a moment or event will prompt a more comprehensive review and redirection in the education system. Change and the need for adaptation are, and will remain, a mainstay in the field of education.

One compelling moment that fundamentally shaped the field of education for an entire generation of educators occurred when President John F. Kennedy spoke the famous words, "Ask not what your country can do for you, ask what you can do for your country." President Kennedy did not direct these words only to teachers, administrators, and education policy makers, but those individuals embraced his words and set out to drive the field of education forward. This early drive to create a better education system is what I believe makes the field of education so dynamic, and for that we should be grateful.

We currently stand on the shoulders of many individuals who came of age professionally in the 1960s, 1970s, and 1980s and inspired by President Kennedy's credo, created the laws, policies, higher education practices, content, assessments, and education services that would benefit students for multiple generations. We must appreciate the importance and impact of these contributions, but we must also recognize that simply continuing the policies and practices in the same manner as they were first created may also lead those currently in the education field toward frustration.

Some teachers and administrators working in the public-school environment today may see a mismatch between what occurred in our public schools long ago and the current school environment. In our modern educational climate, what are we to do? Debate alterations of yesterday's practices and policies? Discard models and approaches developed over decades and completely overhaul the education system? Or do we take an approach that reexamines the theories, approaches, and practices developed in the U.S. education system between the 1960s and 1980s that were a direct result of changes in society as a whole and reinterpret and carry forward the best of these concepts while developing new approaches responsive to this moment? Whatever the decision—stay the course or make a change—we must consider whether President Kennedy's challenge of "doing for our country" is still the ideal goal or is, by itself, a sufficient framework for thinking about the purpose and approach for a public-school education model in the United States entering its third decade of the 2000s.

Many of the cultural, demographic, and broader societal influences impacting our education system and approaches to education have changed dramatically in the 60 years since President Kennedy made his impassioned plea for selflessness and serving a greater purpose. Familial structures, cultural priorities and beliefs, political and policy views, and even the rapid advance in technology and its impact on student learning have all undergone significant changes. Simply taking action for action's sake may not be the best fit for our current environment. We need renewed focus, purpose, and new approaches toward educating our children. Fortunately, we have a rich tapestry of ideas provided by the influential educators and scholars represented in this book we can draw upon and retool various education approaches to meet the needs of generations of students to come. It is paramount for the next generation of educators, administrators, and policy makers to pick up the mantle, adapt what we can, and advance the education system to match the needs of all our students and evolve toward a better future for our children tomorrow.

EVOLUTION BUILT ON A MISSION

> The great aim of education is not knowledge but action.
>
> —Herbert Spencer

Evolution, and its resulting action, doesn't begin and end with an initial drive forward followed by a neutral stasis or complacency. Evolution, at its core, involves constant reflection, modification, and action over time. President Kennedy's statement remains meaningful today because it makes certain tomorrow will evolve differently due to some form of collective action. As Spencer states, we need knowledge and action embedded within our education system. However, I would argue that action is a result of seeing a need for difference. And that difference is the knowledge gained from past experiences and understandings. Because what is action if you don't know where you are headed? What kind of action is possible if you haven't taken into consideration the environments you are confronting moving forward and haven't reflected on those from the past?

ENVIRONMENTAL INFLUENCES ON OUR PUBLIC EDUCATION SYSTEM

In 1961, the field of education was ready for change, but the overall mission for how to educate all students in the United States was unclear. The authors of this book who "came of age" professionally during this time found many challenges to confront and that not all schools were created equal. There was a real need for a comprehensive theory recognizing that the process of learning was different for all children, that we could not overlook those with special needs or gifted tendencies, and that not every child wanted to attend or could afford to pursue education beyond the secondary level. These conclusions became the foundation for many of the policies and practices adopted in the three decades following Kennedy's speech, and they remain a key part of our contemporary education philosophy. But, in recent decades, additional influences and challenges have emerged, making it more difficult to live up to these ideals.

Changing Student Demographics

One current influence on our public educational system is the changing demographics of our student population. As the public schools of the 1960s fought for racial integration, yearly statistics began to be collected both to inform the public and support national education proposals debated on Capitol Hill. Although approximately 89–90% of both white and black children were enrolled in school (per total population; Snyder, 1993), school enrollment for school-age people of color still fell below that of white students. By 2014, that disparity began to decrease (Krogstad & Fry, 2014) and school populations began to show a "minority-majority" trend that is expected to continue. According to the National Center for Education Statistics (NCES), "of the 49.4 million students enrolled in public elementary and secondary schools in fall 2020, some 22.6 million were White, 13.8 million were Hispanic, 7.4 million were Black, 2.7 million were Asian, 2.2 million were of Two or more races, 0.5 million were American Indian/Alaska Native, and 180,000 were Pacific Islander" (2022, para. 2). These recent statistics indicate a real difference in the racial, ethnic, and cultural composition of the classrooms in the public-school environment compared to the 1960s.

Increased Internet Access, Reliability, and Influence

A second, more current influence on our public-school students is the increased access and reliability on the internet both as an education tool and in the lives of children outside of school. In 2019, 92% of children ages 3 to 18 had access to the internet via a computer or smartphone (NCES, 2022). Originally thought to allow computers to "speak" to each other using the same language, internet developers of the 1980s clearly could not anticipate how this platform would be used and accessed by younger individuals. In fall 2001, 99% of public schools in the United States had access to the internet (NCES, 2002–2018). As much as access to the internet has improved student learning potential, internet use by children and teens remains heavily influenced by apps, videos, gaming, and direct messaging and texting with friends. According to the Common Sense Census (CSC; 2021), tweens entertainment screen usage is approximately 5 hours and 33 minutes per day. Teens clock in at 8 hours and 39 minutes per day. This is a 20% and 28% increase, respectively, since 2015 (CSC, 2021). Watching TV/videos (approximately three hours per day) takes top priority, with gaming (1½ hours/day), browsing websites (24–50 minutes/day), and social media (18 minutes–1½ hours/day) as the many ways tweens and teens use the internet (CSC, 2021). Increased internet usage dominated by media watching directly influences how students view overall internet use and that may shift overall internet use in schools for instructional purposes as well as the teaching strategies used to teach the internet to students.

Overall internet use is not the only influence on students currently. It is also important to know what students are watching when using this technology. In 2021, the most popular app was YouTube (32% of weekly use), followed by SnapChat (20% of weekly use; CSC, 2012). Experts caution that unmonitored internet use, especially for younger children, can promote viewing graphic, scary, and/or explicit content. Further, "misinformation is rife on social media platforms like YouTube" (Moyer, 2022, para. 16). Young children may have difficulty identifying what content is real and what might be fake, therefore creating a confusing reality of the world for them. In addition, two-thirds of U.S. teens follow some kind of influencer (gaming, music, fashion, etc.; YouGov, 2021), thus coloring their view of the world even further or creating different views about what is or what should be valued compared to students of the pre-internet and smart phone generation. Social media influencers are individuals with "an online following based on their personality, skills, or interests." In addition, "influencers often share snippets of their everyday lives and activities, . . . tend to have large audiences and often create sponsored content around products to spur sales—and make money" (Zapal, 2022, paras. 3 and 4). Influencers can provide a positive platform for entertainment, social activism, and well-being. However, similar to unmonitored overall internet use, influencers may also expose younger children to unhealthy themes and products, create comparisons between young followers and the "perfect" life of the influencer, and promote an unhealthy ideal body, type, gender, or cultural image for young children to follow or aspire to be. Regardless of whether one believes the net impact of the heavy online content consumption and social media is beneficial, there is an impact on the beliefs, values, and priorities of students in the classroom as well as a host of additional administrative impacts including dealing with cyber bullying.

The Politicization of Education and the Education System

The hyper-politicization of education is a third influence on our public education system that we must recognize has impacts in the classroom, at the administrative level, and in local communities. Inherently ingrained into our public education system are mores based upon systems, beliefs, attitudes, and values of those individuals and groups of individuals who surround the public-school building. In theory, our democratic ideals would allow these individuals (and groups) with different viewpoints and understandings the ability to create a space where conversation remains open, listening skills are at a premium, and compromise reigns supreme. Acting in this manner should result in positive outcomes for the students who also reside within this space. However, this utopian idea only perseveres when the purpose of public education is "to give the young the things they need to develop in an orderly, sequential way into members of society . . . [because] Any education is, in its forms and methods, an outgrowth of the needs of the society in which it exists" (Dewey, 1934, p. 1). In short, utopia only exists in our minds but rarely in our everyday actions.

Many different actors influence our U.S. education system including the government (including those individuals directly related to the educational system) and nongovernment actors such as interest groups, policy organizations, the media, and the general public (Fowler, 2013). Each actor is constantly positioning to influence or benefit from the education system. Why? As the education of our young children remains a public service for all with decisions, commitments, and actions to be interpreted by various stakeholders, our education system sits directly in the middle of public policy.

When public policy "includes both official enactments of government and something as informal as 'practices'" (Cibulka, 1995, p. 106), it can become political. "What is taught and how it is taught is shaped by the cultural, social, political, and historical contexts in which a school is situated" (Walker, 2018, para. 8) do not always remain neutral. Often, they are ripe with action and in response to the many changing and evolving environments around them. Therefore, the textbooks, curriculum, policies, and practices used in our educational system are inherently political. Not surprisingly, teachers, principals, superintendents, and other school leaders "find themselves in the middle of heated disputes" (Fowler, 2013, p. 115) surrounding ideological conflicts in public schools.

Although historically political issues have always shadowed and impacted the public-school system, including integration and busing, many other contemporary issues such as the existence of mass communication platforms including social media magnify, intensify, and amplify the decision making of schools and school boards. The same platforms have contributed to a broader corrosion in our national political debate and have, regrettably, brought differences in cultural values on national issues down to the level of the schoolhouse. This space is often where confrontations between education professionals, parents, and interest groups occur about what children should be taught, when, and by whom. Misinformation or partial information also spreads rapidly through these technology platforms and can further intensify these debates, all of which have an impact on teacher and administrator attitudes toward education and their willingness to continue in the profession. We must recognize that any pedagogy, whether adapted and carried forward from prior eras or newly developed, will be scrutinized and potentially politicized to a much greater degree than in prior generations.

Various Teaching Theories and Approaches: A Survival Guide

The final influence on our public education system that we need to consider are our theories and approaches to teaching students. Teacher pedagogy is ripe with various means toward learning and instruction including (and this is not an exhaustive list):

- concept formation (Bruner),
- "following the child" (Montessori),
- developmental stages of thought (Piaget),
- sociocultural development of cognition based upon social interactions (Vygotsky),
- curriculum development based upon student needs (Taba),

- multiple-intelligence theory (Gardner), and
- differentiation of instruction (Tomlinson).

These theories and approaches (among others) have circulated throughout schools of education for many years, thus permeating our public-school classrooms. However, educators and administrators are often left feeling inundated by various theory-to-practice directives from outside sources (textbook companies, national educational policies, private monetary resources, etc.) that seem to be constantly changing. This struggle for consensus, consistency, and time needed to see the theory to fruition sometimes creates a feeling of merely trying to survive the many demands placed upon them rather than having the time to ensure proper implementation that will lead to positive educational outcomes for students.

STANDING ON THEIR SHOULDERS

We should not consider the lived experiences and perspectives of the authors in this book as merely historical reflections just because our student demographics have changed or because access to and reliance on the internet, including how our young people navigate current influencers, has increased. Nor can these valuable perspectives be set aside because the politicization of education policy and practice has intensified. As the development of theory and practice over multiple decades in response to specific societal factors has shifted, these chapters continue to offer fertile ground for study and potential adaption to new challenges. In fact, as pioneers in this systemic process, the authors may hold the keys necessary to tackle current educational challenges. The authors knew that the true test of fulfilling President Kennedy's profound and complicated mission of educating all our children lay in creating and putting into place systems and policies that would guarantee that educating all children would be more than a goal. The mission would become a guarantee for all students when they walked through the door each school day. It is up to current educators, school administrators, and policy makers to draw from the past experiences of others to pave a path for the future of our students.

Current educational challenges in broadening classroom curriculum to ensure inclusivity, bridging the disconnect between generations within our educational system to better tackle real learning, and raising the bar for the entire education system including accreditation of programs and teachers becoming leaders in their schools can draw directly from the authors' experiences and their written chapters. Here I will offer some insight from the authors as well as engage in conversation about the current system and its future.

K–12 Educational Practice: Teaching Algebra to All

Early American educational practice included the study of algebra. Spielhagen outlined many reasons why policy makers over time redirected the study of algebra to a smaller, select population of wealthy, college-bound, high-school students. These reasons include a rise in immigrant populations in urban settings, increased industrialization and job opportunities, students leaving public school systems well before graduation, and shifting economics fostering inequity of education attainment. With shifts in worker skill requirements, the modern workplace, and the need for critical thinking and problem solving in many aspects of daily living, the practice of marginalizing algebra in public schools is something we need to question.

Once part of the grammar school curriculum, eliminating algebra until a student reached a particular point in his high-school career, "caused the elite status of the study of algebra to be not only a barrier to college entrance, but also to full citizenship and economic autonomy in the U.S." (Spielhagen, as cited in Moses & Cobb, 2000). But it remains as true as ever that not all students will attend college or university. Indeed, post pandemic, fewer students are willing to take on higher education debt to attend college. Further, employers have begun instead to change their demands for degrees in many occupations and job opportunities offering various routes toward employment. Nevertheless, the U.S. Bureau of Labor Statistics (2021) states that employment in STEM occupations (for college- and noncollege-educated workers) has grown 79% in the past three decades and is expected to grow 11% more between 2020 and 2030. Mathematics instruction, such as algebra, increases students' ability to think critically, spot patterns, work backwards, visualize, work systematically, and use logical reasoning (University of Leeds, 2019). This makes it more critical than ever for all students to be ready to think critically, solve problems, and embrace complex tasks. Segregating math offerings between college-bound students and those students seeking direct employment without ensuring that the broader math curriculum, like teaching algebra, will not prepare all students for the 21st century workplace and society. It is absolutely the wrong way to go. The theoretical basis for ensuring broad student access to mathematics and critical thinking and problem-solving coursework is as appropriate and applicable as ever, even with all the changes noted previously.

Forging a Bridge

U.S. public-school teachers, administrators, and policy makers must take into account ethnic diversity of student populations when considering teaching and learning strategies in public schools. In addition, Sobel notes financial challenges, staffing, dynamic changes in education mandates and curriculum, and evolving educator professional development all shift as national student and family demographics also change. Adding these criteria creates a challenging classroom environment to teach all content topics. Educators, school administrators, and policy makers must use a variety of teaching and learning approaches to create a positive, productive learning environment for all students.

Cultural and racial diversity are not the only descriptors that should concern educators, administrators, and policy makers. Baldwin presents the progression of special education from one of inadequacy and shame toward a more thorough understanding of inclusive and individualized services "tailored to meet the student's educational and social/emotional needs." Increased research has added much to the field of special education, specifically the subfield of autism spectrum disorders (ASD). We now understand that 1 in 44 children from all racial, ethnic, and socioeconomic groups has been identified with ASD (Maenner, Shaw, Bakian, et al., 2021). However, as McMahon reminded us, "dozens and dozens of traits and idiosyncratic characteristics of children with ASD" (p. 135) further complicate our mission of educating all children. Observation and staying ahead of current research will provide educators, administrators, and policy makers information about how best to serve and teach these identified students. But making an intentional effort to speak with families about their children is crucial toward forging a bridge between families and schools. Because "understanding these characteristics [of students identified with ASD] will help support academic and social success for students and be very helpful in designing motivational strategies and positive learning environments" (p. 66). With expected further improvements in the research base and diagnostic capabilities, the relevance of Baldwin and McMahon remains highly applicable as the population of differently abled students in heterogeneous classrooms continues to grow.

Reis defines her intellectual journey as one of "self-selected creative work" without the support of her teachers, administrators, and educational policies. The concept of understanding how to teach and train the minds of the gifted and talented did not take precedence until the fall of 1963. In response to the space race with Russia, educators, administrators, and policy makers scrambled to ensure that "the best and the brightest" were put to the test academically. However, what we knew of high-ability students then juxtaposed with what we understand to be now mimics the field of special education in attitude and research. Many, both inside and outside the field of education, thought bright students to "be fine on their own" and need little, if any, academic, social, or emotional support. Yet research shows us that identification of these students is and remains complicated. Best practices for identifying and nurturing gifted potential in all student populations requires much more than a standardized assessment given on a few days during the previous school year. Françoys Gagné (1985) encouraged a focus on talent development. This may have been the catalyst toward a change in the definition of gifted and talented individuals (NAGC, 2018) to incorporate the potential for talent (based upon a particular field of study) and fully integrate identification procedures for all students, including those from diverse ethnic and economic backgrounds (Bernal, 2002; Frasier & Passow, 1994; Van Tassel-Baska, Johnson, & Avery, 2002). Current educators, administrators, and policy makers are also now aware of students who are identified in need of gifted and talented education services and special education services. We continue to work toward serving twice-exceptional (2e) students through various federal legislation, grants, and funding directed at public school systems.

Sobel's "meeting students where they are" mantra remains applicable to today's students; however, where students are has changed. "The baby boomers used their learned sense of culture, community, and family to create structurally sound educational institutions for their children and future generations to come" (p. 10). This directive is commendable and, arguably, should also apply to today's educational climate. In fact, the increase in research studies and information on teaching socioemotional learning (SEL), broadening the scope of the familial unit in America, offering less homework, emphasizing play/recess, and the uptick in extracurricular activity among students shows that current educators, administrators, and policy makers still value student culture, community, and families as key components to "educating the whole child." As previously noted, our students are in different places in their lives than in the 1960s. Increased women's rights, available contraception, and the Equal Pay Act of 1963 increased the number of women in the U.S. workforce (Walsh, 2010). This led to more working mothers, additional children in day care/after-school activities, changes in familial structures including an increase in single-parent households, and a more equal distribution of household chores and child rearing by men and women (Blau & Winkler, 2017). Other changes in familial economic conditions, increased immigration into the United States, varying crime rates, technological advances, health-care advantages and disadvantages, increased costs of housing, food, and transportation expenses all relate (directly and indirectly) to our changing student demographics and how they attend and perform in school.

One important point from Sobel's chapter lies in recognizing the possible disconnect between those currently in the field of education and their personal views on culture, community, and family and the students' views on these same topics. Although a student-centered approach to education has proven beneficial, that point of education where true learning can take place isn't the same for all students. Therefore, current educators, administrators, and policy makers must work diligently and adjust their thinking about learning in general to figure out the "sweet spot" of teaching all children. Zeichner, Bowman, Guillen, and Napolitan (2016) suggest that when teachers know about the communities in which their students reside, these teachers can "make use of this knowledge and these relationships to support their students' learning" (Lui & Ball, 2019, p. 81). The InTASC Model Standard 10 also states that teachers should "take responsibility . . . to collaborate with learners, families, colleagues, other school professionals, and community members to ensure learner growth" (Council of Chief State School Officers, 2013). Learning about and using student background information not only engages students more in the overall learning process, but it creates a more developmentally appropriate and flexible learning environment, which ultimately leads to overall positive learning growth outcomes (Osterman, 2000).

Sobel's goal of educating all children may remain highly appropriate, but the means to that end will definitely require refinement to existing theories and development of new ones to make this goal realistic in our current education climate. "Meeting all students where they are is a commitment that requires that we reconfigure our old systems and practices and paradigms; that we place the individual learner at the center of the learning process; and that the learning process—what actually happens cognitively, neurologically, and developmentally as children learn—be placed at the center of the pedagogical model" (Rudenstine, Schaef, & Bacallao, 2017, p. 2). Three driving questions prove relevant toward this end:

- How do we know where students are?
- What do we do once we know? and
- Which strategies help us navigate systemic constraints? (Rudenstine, Schaef, & Bacallao, 2017)

Allowing our public schools to be places of structured flexibility can help respond to many challenges in our education system. Reimagining and redesigning our schools using different scheduling practices, assessments, increased project- and problem-based learning opportunities, modular and more personalized learning experiences, and supports for learning that foster student agency, motivation, and engagement can bridge the gap between the older and younger generations of individuals within our public-school systems.

Raising the Bar for Teachers and the Educational System

Our current education system in the United States remains an integral part of our overall country's health and well-being. The "American dream" for many people involves hard work and becoming educated. DiSalvo discusses education "at the center" of the neighborhood in which he lived: "In a community with so many moving parts, education was always at the center" (p. 99). Whether part of a neighborhood school in an urban environment or a small, multigrade school building in a rural state, educators and administrators are at the epicenter of the education system.

Properly trained educators and administrators are crucial for an education system to thrive. Cibulka discusses his role in "an interlocking reform strategy—stronger national accreditation, a better system of teacher preparation, and a better sourcing and supply of well-qualified teachers." Due to increased federal legislation including the No Child Left Behind Act (NCLB) of 2001 and its reauthorization, Every Child Succeeds Act (ESSA) of 2015, accountability of teacher-preparation programs at the collegiate level rose to new heights. As a result, the National Council for the Accreditation of Teacher Education (NCATE) and the American Association of College of Teacher Education (AACTE) worked diligently to create and maintain systemic changes in the way we prepare educators and the institutions that house this process. But this process has, and continues to be, riddled with challenges. Despite the hardships, Cibulka maintains,

> to a remarkable degree, albeit on a narrower scale, CAEP's challenges illustrate a fundamental crisis confronting our nation: how to restore effectiveness and support for our public-serving institutions. While there is no consensus on how this renewal can be accomplished, a strategy of indifference or inaction would be a serious, potentially fatal, mistake. (p. 121)

Our current education system has a possibly even bigger challenge: a national teacher shortage. Post pandemic, many teachers are leaving their classrooms in search of different employment opportunities. Similar to Bassett and Stewart's research, teachers today are leaving the profession because of "lack of feedback and interest in teacher growth by administration, lack of recognition of their excellence, and lack of teacher leader opportunities" (p. 14). According to the most recent Title II report (U.S. Department of Education, 2022), students enrolled in teacher preparation programs have dropped by more than 150,000 in two years—a 19% decrease from the 2012–2013 school year to the 2018–2019 school year (p. 2). Affording current educators additional resources for leadership opportunities in the form of professional development training may not be enough. Educators and administrators are retiring (some of them earlier than anticipated for a variety of reasons), causing schools to lose roughly a million and a half veteran teachers to retirement during the next eight years (from 2010 to 2018; NCTAF, 2010). Another statistic for consideration is the working ideals of the current generation. According to the Department of Labor (2021), a worker will hold an average of 11.7 different jobs between the ages of 18 and 48. How will we recover and move forward from this massive shortfall?

One micro solution: engaging and increased teacher leadership for those currently in the field. According to Bassett and Stewart, the teacher leadership model standards (TLMS) of 2011 were created to support teachers and "to stimulate dialogue among stakeholders of the teaching profession about what constitutes the knowledge, skills, and competencies that teachers need to assume leadership roles in their schools, districts, and the profession" (Teacher Leadership Exploratory Consortium, 2011, p. 3). Maybe more important, however, the TLMS gave educators a roadmap and mission of support strategies and learning behaviors linked to increased student achievement and breaking the status quo of mediocrity in student learning, both now and into the future. Teacher leadership would come directly from teachers in classrooms, using data collected from their students in real time. Sustained change and dissemination of relevant knowledge and skills to best serve students would reside from within. Bassett and Stewart maintain that developing teacher leaders who remain in the profession for the long term consistently supports student growth and academic development and may keep current teachers in our classrooms for the long haul.

Recent alternative teacher certification programs such as Teach for America and Teachers of Tomorrow help recruit and train more diverse individuals to become teachers, often at an advanced rate. Similarly, teacher-preparation programs affiliated or located within higher education schools offer certification programs specific to those active in the U.S. military who want to serve their country in the classroom after active duty. As novice teachers are entering into our public-school classrooms at a more rapid rate (although not quite enough to fill the current demand), we must carefully consider how these programs will become and remain accredited and comparable to those already established programs in higher education institutions. It is not enough to fill a quota of individuals missing in the education system. Rather, steps created by educators, administrators, and policy makers of today will be necessary to maintain high standards and quality across all these efforts. The collective experiences of those who worked hard to promote preservice teaching standards and teacher quality are critical to ensure that we fill massive vacancies through new and existing training and certification programs without sacrificing quality and effectiveness.

CONCLUSION

Current educators, administrators, and policy makers stand on the shoulders of past individuals who took John F. Kennedy's directive so many years ago. If President Kennedy's challenge of "doing for our country" is still the ideal goal, we must consider whether to make changes to our current system, have some directives remain the same, or a combination of both that match our current education climate and move us forward into another century. As a result of the familial, cultural, political, policy, and technological environments that have changed in the past 60 years, I encourage those of us in the current educational environments to consider which, if any, of the principles, philosophies, theories, and techniques pioneered by our authors can be reused and deployed moving forward in pursuit of Kennedy's ideal.

New challenges face our educational system. Our students are culturally, ethnically, economically, and academically different from students in the 1960s, 1970s, and even the 1980s. Our students will require skill sets for jobs unknown to us in the present day. We are better able to identify student academic, emotional, and social needs than we were before. But with additional information and research, more specified and differentiated theories, approaches to teaching and learning, and sets of skills must be used and taught to our current and future students. Apple (1999) states, "the recognition that schools—and the curricula, teaching, and evaluative policies and practices that structure the daily events that go on in them—are among the most central of our institutionalized sets of social relations is not new, of course. But our understanding of what this means has grown massively [over the past decade]" (p. 3). Because of our growth and understanding of education and teaching, this directive requires highly trained educators and administrators who are equipped for the challenge. Our students are demanding better, and we need to respond with better.

It would be impossible to detail every change to the American education system moving forward; however, a few necessities come to my mind. First, we need to increase civics education in our public schools. On December 22, 2022, Congress appropriated $23 million to improve civics and history education nationally (CivXNow, 2022). This bipartisan legislation, a first in decades, will allocate $3 million for the already existing American history and civics academies and an additional $20 million for a competitive grant program, "Civics National Activities" for eligible institutions using evidence-based practices "to improv[e] teaching and learning about the history and principles of the Constitution of the United States" (CivXNow, 2022, para. 2). Our education system and the ideas about schooling are based on civics education as we know it from Horace Mann. As the "father of

American education," Mann argued that "free, standardized, and universal schooling was essential to the grand American experiment of self-governance" (Winthrop, 2020, para. 6), and it was this universal schooling that helped teach of the ideals, issues, and challenges facing our new nation and that of its future.

Civics education reaches farther than one class in high school. According to CivXNow, civics education is composed of three ideals: knowledge and skills, values and dispositions, and behaviors. Civics education offers students the ability to:

1. gain an understanding of the processes of government, prevalent political ideologies, civic and constitutional rights, and the history and heritage of the above;
2. gain an appreciation for civil discourse, free speech, and engaging with those whose perspectives differ from their own; and
3. develop the civic agency and confidence to vote, volunteer, attend public meetings, and engage with their communities.

In the words of Chief Justice John Roberts, "Civic education, like all education, is a continuing enterprise and conversation. Each generation has an obligation to pass on to the next, not only a fully functioning government responsive to the needs of the people, but the tools to understand and improve it" (Roberts, 2019, p. 4).

Second, I believe in teaching students through critical thinking and problem-finding and -problem-solving initiatives. Critical thinking involves more than teaching students how to analyze scientific data. The critical-thinking community defines critical thinking as "the intellectually disciplined process of actively and skillfully conceptualizing, applying, analyzing, synthesizing, and/or evaluating information gathered from, or generated by, observation, experience, reflection, reasoning, or communication, as a guide to belief and action" (Scriven & Paul, 2007, p. 1). Critical-thinking skills are important because they enable students "to deal effectively with social, scientific, and practical problems" (Shakirova, 2007, p. 42). When students can think critically, they are also able to make decisions and solve problems effectively. This skill is paramount in school, the workplace, and in their personal lives.

Problem-finding and problem-solving teaching and learning strategies are the result of problem-based learning theory (PBL). PBL is a learner-centered instructional method in which students work collaboratively and learn through solving ill-structured problems (Barrows, 2000; Hmelo-Silver, 2004; Torp & Sage, 2002). PBL is often self-directed, with the teacher acting as a facilitator rather than a provider of knowledge. The learning is embedded within a PBL problem (Gallagher, Stepien, & Rosenthal, 1992) and formulated through student discussions (Schmidt, DeVolder, DeGrave, Moust, & Patel, 1989), therefore mapping new knowledge onto previously understood knowledge. Through the process of PBL, students can practice thinking critically about and solving problems—all skills helpful to them and their futures.

Finally, we need to teach students how to increase their personal and global perspectives. Socioemotional learning (SEL) is the process of understanding emotions and how they help us to think, feel, and behave (Coskun, 2019). It is crucial to manage and regulate our emotions because lacking this skill can result in "excessive, inappropriate, and insufficient responses to environmental and situational demands" (p. 764). Over time, increased SEL helps students graduate, be ready for postsecondary education, increase career success, maintain positive family and work relationships, provide overall better mental health, reduce criminal behavior, and increase civic engagement (Hawkins, Kosterman, Catalano, Hill, & Abbott, 2008; Jones, Greenberg, & Crowley, 2015). All these traits will help students understand themselves and relate better to other people throughout their lives.

In hindsight, President Kennedy must have known that the more difficult missions, such as educating all U.S. children, were not to be left to passive observers. This challenging mission needed active participants to determine and set a course unknown while reflecting, learning, fixing, and modifying that course as it moves forward. The authors of this book knew that the true test of fulfilling such a vast, complicated mission of educating all our children was to create and put into place systems and policies that support that mission. They began to chart a course from that previously unknown. Each chapter in this book has outlined, and often defined for the first time, various needs to support and educate every child to become their best self through various aspects of K–12 education, higher education, and teacher education. For the authors, these needs came from personal experiences, family and neighborhood cultures, and self-created positions in the field, and those currently in the field must not forget the paths forged before us. I am grateful to each author of this book for deciding to take on this mission—however difficult it proved to be. We can continue to understand their contributions both as historical achievements and contributions and as a basis for meeting the challenges confronting the next generation of educators.

Although components within the field of education continue to evolve and be debated over time, one element in the field remains steadfast: educators, administrators, and policy makers are the gatekeepers for all students to learn, thrive, grow, and become themselves, or arguably, their best selves. I believe the future of our country and our world depends upon the education of each child—the whole child. Asking not how our country is going to educate our children but how we will continue to educate each child to become their best selves is indeed at the core of every author in this book, including me. The great task of educating our children in evolving and uncertain times, however, lies in continuing to ask questions about how we will accomplish this goal. What an educator does in teaching is to make it possible for students to become "beings for themselves" (Freire, 2005, p. 74).

REFERENCES

Apple, M. W. (1999). Chapter 1: The personal and the political in critical educational studies. *Counterpoints, 109*, 3–27.

Barrows, H. S. (2000). *Problem-based learning applied to medical education.* Southern Illinois University Press.

Bernal, E. M. (2002). Three ways to achieve a more equitable representation of culturally and linguistically different students in GT programs. *Roeper Review, 24*, 82–88.

Blau, F. D., & Winkler, A. E. (2017). *Women, work, and family.* National Bureau of Economic Research. https://www.nber.org/system/files/working_papers/w23644/w23644.pdf

Cibulka, J. G. (1995). Policy analysis and the study of politics of education. In J. D. Scriber & D. Layton (Eds.), *The study of educational politics* (pp. 105–125). Falmer Press.

CivXNow. (2022, December 23). *Press release: Civic education receives significant boost, as federal lawmakers appropriate $23 million in last-minute omnibus bill.* https://civxnow.org/press-release-civic-education-receives-significant-boost-as-federal-lawmakers-appropriate-23-million-in-last-minute-omnibus-bill/

Coskun, K. (2019). Evaluation of the socio emotional learning (SEL) activities on self-regulation skills among primary school children. *Qualitative Report, 24*(4), 764–780.

Council of Chief State School Officers. (2013). *InTASC model core teaching standards and learning progressions for teachers 1.0.* Washington, DC: Author. https://ccsso.org/sites/default/files/2017-12/2013_INTASC_Learning_Progressions_for_Teachers.pdf

Dewey, John. (1934). Individual psychology and education. *The Philosopher, 12*(1), 1–6.

Fowler, F. C. (2013). *Policy studies for educational leaders: An introduction.* Pearson.

Frasier, M. M., & Passow, A. H. (1994). Toward a new paradigm for identifying talent potential. Storrs: National Research Center on the Gifted and Talented, University of Connecticut.

Frayer, S., Lacey, A., & Watson, A. (2017, January). *STEM occupations: Past, present, and future.* https://www.bls.gov/spotlight/2017/science-technology-engineering-and-mathematics-stem-occupations-past-present-and-future/home.htm

Freire, P. (2005). *Pedagogy of the oppressed.* The Continuum International Publishing Group.

Gagné, F. (1985). Giftedness and talent: Reexamining a reexamination of the definitions. *Gifted Child Quarterly, 29*(3), 103–112.

Gallagher, S. A., Stepien, W. J., & Rosenthal, H. (1992). The effects of problem-based learning on problem-solving. *Gifted Child Quarterly, 36*, 195–200.

Hawkins, J. D., Kosterman, R., Catalano, R. F., Hill, K. G., & Abbott, R. D. (2008). Effects of social development intervention in childhood 15 years later. *Archives of Pediatrics & Adolescent Medicine, 162*(12), 1133–1141.

Hmelo-Silver, C. E. (2004). Problem-based learning: What and how do students learn? *Educational Psychology Review, 16*, 235–266.

Jones, D. E., Greenberg, M., & Crowley, M. (2015). Early social-emotional functioning and public health: The relationship between kindergarten social competence and future wellness. *American Journal of Public Health, 105*(11), 2283–2290.

Kleiner, A., & Farris, E. (2002). *Internet access in U.S. public schools and classrooms: 1994–2001.* U.S. Department of Education, National Center for Education Statistics (NCES). https://nces.ed.gov/pubs2002/2002018.pdf

Liu, K., & Ball, A. F. (2019). Critical reflection and generativity: Toward a framework of transformative teacher education for diverse learners. *Review of Research in Education, 43*(1), 68–105. https://doi.org/10.3102/0091732X18822806

Krogstad, J. M., & Fry, R. (2014, August 18). *Dept. of Ed. projects public schools will be "majority-minority" this fall.* Pew Research Center. https://www.pewresearch.org/fact-tank/2014/08/18/u-s-public-schools-expected-to-be-majority-minority-starting-this-fall/

Maenner, M. J., Shaw, K. A., Bakian, A. V., et al. (2021). *Prevalence and characteristics of autism spectrum disorder among children aged 8 years—Autism and developmental disabilities monitoring network, 11 sites, United States, 2018.* Centers for Disease Control and Prevention. https://www.cdc.gov/mmwr/volumes/70/ss/ss7011a1.htm

MarketingCharts. (2021, December 6). *2 in 3 U.S. teens follow influencers. Which types are most popular?* MarketingCharts. https://www.marketingcharts.com/industries/media-and-entertainment-119129#:~:text=Per%20a%20recent%20report%20%5Bdownload,63%25%20of%20US%20male%20teens

Moses, B., & Cobb, C. (2000). *Radical equations: Math, literacy, and civil rights.* Beacon Press.

Moyer, M. W. (2022, March 24). Kids as young as 8 are using social media more than ever, study finds. *New York Times.* https://www.nytimes.com/2022/03/24/well/family/child-social-media-use.html

NAGC white paper. (2018). https://cdn.ymaws.com/nagc.org/resource/resmgr/knowledge-center/position-statements/Task_Force_Report_Gifted_Def.pdf

National Center for Education Statistics (NCES). (2022). *Children's internet access at home.* https://nces.ed.gov/programs/coe/indicator/cch

National Center for Education Statistics (NCES). (2022). *Racial/ethnic enrollment in public schools.* https://nces.ed.gov/programs/coe/indicator/cge

National Commission on Teaching and America's Future (NCTAF). (2010). *Who will teach? Experience matters.* https://files.eric.ed.gov/fulltext/ED511985.pdf

Osterman, K. F. (2000). Students' need for belonging in the school community. *Review of Educational Research, 70*, 323–367.

Roberts, J. (2019). *2019-Year-End Report on the Federal Judiciary*. https://www.supremecourt.gov/publicinfo/year-end/2019year-endreport.pdf

Rudenstine, A., Schaef, S., & Bacallao, D. (2017). *Meeting students where they are*. Aurora Institute. https://www.aurora-institute.org/wp-content/uploads/CompetencyWorks-MeetingStudentsWhereTheyAre2.pdf

Schmidt, H. G., DeGrave, W. S., DeVolder, M. L., Moust, J. H. C., & Patel, V. L. (1989). Explanatory models in the processing of science text: The role of prior knowledge activation through small group discussion. *Journal of Educational Psychology, 81*, 610–619.

Scriven, M., & Paul, R. (2007). *Defining critical thinking*. The Critical Thinking Community: Foundation for Critical Thinking. http://www.criticalthinking.org/aboutCT/define_critical_thinking.cfm

Shakirova, D. M. (2007). Technology for the shaping of college students' and upper-grade students' critical thinking. *Russian Education & Society, 49*(9), 42–52.

Snyder, T. D. (1993). *120 years of American education: A statistical portrait*. U.S. Department of Education: Office of Educational Research and Improvement, National Center for Education Statistics. https://nces.ed.gov/pubs93/93442.pdf

The Teacher Leadership Exploratory Consortium. (2011). *The teacher leader model standards*. https://www.education.udel.edu/wp-content/uploads/2013/07/Exploratory-Consortium.pdf

Torp, L., & Sage, S. (2002). *Problems as possibilities*. ASCD.

University of Leeds. (2019, September 1). *4 reasons to study mathematics*. Leeds International Study Centre. https://www.leedsisc.com/news/why-study-mathematics

U.S. Department of Education: Office of Postsecondary Education. (2022). *Preparing and credentialing the nation's teachers the secretary's report on the teacher workforce*. https://title2.ed.gov/Public/OPE%20Annual%20Report.pdf

U.S. Department of Labor: Bureau of Statistics. (2021). *Number of jobs, labor market experience, marital status, and health: Results from a national longitudinal survey*. https://www.bls.gov/news.release/pdf/nlsoy.pdf

Van Tassel-Baska, J., Johnson, D., & Avery, L. (2002). Using performance tasks in the identification of economically disadvantaged and minority gifted learners: Findings from project star. *Gifted Child Quarterly, 46*, 110–123.

Walker, T. (2018, December 18). *"Education is political": Neutrality in the classroom shortchanges students*. National Education Association. https://www.nea.org/advocating-for-change/new-from-nea/education-political-neutrality-classroom-shortchanges-students

Walsh, K. T. (2010, March 12). *The 1960s: A decade of change for women*. U.S. News. https://www.usnews.com/news/articles/2010/03/12/the-1960s-a-decade-of-change-for-women

Winthrop, R. (2020, June 4). *The need for civic education in 21st century schools*. Policy 2020. https://www.brookings.edu/policy2020/bigideas/the-need-for-civic-education-in-21st-century-schools/

Zapal, H. (2022, November 2). *Social media influencers' impact on youth today.* Bark Blog. https://www.bark.us/blog/social-media-influencers/

Zeichner, K., Bowman, M., Guillen, L., & Napolitan, K. (2016). Engaging and working in solidarity with local communities in preparing the teachers of their children. *Journal of Teacher Education, 67*(4), 277–290. https://doi.org/10.1177/0022487116660623

About the Editors and Contributors

Frances Spielhagen earned a doctorate in educational leadership and policy from Fordham University in 2002. She was a teacher in 7–12 schools in New York and New Jersey for more than 30 years, with teaching certificates in Latin, English, social studies, and gifted education. After earning her doctorate, she earned a three-year postdoctoral research fellowship from the American Educational Research Association, which sponsored her research in equity and access in mathematics. That research resulted in the book *The Algebra Solution to Mathematics Reform* (2011). She has also written scholarly articles and books on adolescent development and single-sex education, as well as on pedagogy. She wrote *Pedagogy into Practice: A Handbook for New Teachers* (2020) in conjunction with a former student and now teaching colleague. She was editor of the *Middle Grades Research Journal*. Dr. Spielhagen is professor emerita at Mount Saint Mary College in Newburgh, New York, where she taught teacher candidates for 20 years.

Paige Hendricks, PhD, is an educational consultant, curriculum writer, and professional development content creator and presenter for various public and private schools, universities, and educational organizations nationally. She writes and presents high-quality, in-person, and online educational resources that translate research into practice for special and general education teachers, faculty, and current education students. Her research interests and consulting work specialize in curriculum writing, instruction, and assessment; student and teacher multiculturalism in school settings; twice-exceptionality; and preservice/veteran teacher training modules and initiatives in differentiated instruction and problem-based learning. Hendricks also hosts a podcast called *Get Off the Dotted Line!*, which unpacks all things related to education and teaching to help elementary teachers think differently about what they are teaching and why they are teaching it to create classroom spaces for amazing learning potential to begin. Hendricks was a visiting assistant professor at William and Mary, where she taught courses in elementary and secondary social studies methods, instruction, and assessment to preservice education students. She also served as an adjunct faculty member and guest lecturer at three Virginia higher education institutions teaching courses in social studies methods, educational instruction and assessment, foundations in education, introduction to teaching, and gifted education. Hendricks has worked in a variety of public, nonprofit, and for-profit educational settings in multiple states, in-person, and online. She resides in Williamsburg, Virginia, with her husband and academically talented and creative son.

***

Lois Baldwin, EdD, was both a teacher and an administrator of one of the first programs in the country serving 2e students. She has assisted teachers and staff with curriculum development, student issues, transition planning, assessment, and professional development and is still doing so for various local districts in New York. She cofounded the Association for the Education of Gifted Underachieving students (AEGUS) and served as the president. Dr. Baldwin has taught courses on giftedness and twice exceptionality at Manhattanville College, Pace University, College of New Rochelle, and Regis University, and has been a consultant and speaker at numerous national conferences and symposiums. She consulted for the Colorado Department of Education Twice Exceptional Project, where she helped to design and present an online course, workshops, training modules, manuals, and materials for educators throughout the state. In addition, she has coauthored several professional articles and chapters. She is on the advisory board of GiftedNYS.

Katherine Bassett, EdM, is chief executive officer of the New Jersey Tutoring Corps. The New Jersey State Teacher of the Year 2000, Bassett spent 26 years as a middle-school librarian on a barrier island in southeastern New Jersey. She has served in a leadership capacity at both ETS and Pearson, cofounded and served as inaugural president and CEO of the National Network of State Teachers of the Year, and has run her own education consulting company, Tall Poppy. Bassett is the lead developer of the teacher leader model standards, colead developer of the model code of ethics for educators, and principal researcher on more than 15 research studies.

James G. Cibulka holds a PhD from the University of Chicago with concentrations in educational administration and political science. He held professorial and administrative appointments at the University of Wisconsin-Milwaukee (UWM), the University of Maryland, and the University of Kentucky, where he served as dean of the College of Education. His scholarship focuses on educational leadership, urban education reform, community empowerment, and school finance reform. In addition, he has addressed redesign of educator preparation programs in higher education. He founded a Department of Community Education at UWM. Between 2008 and 2015, he was president of the National Council for the Accreditation of Teacher Education (NCATE) and most recently, the Council for the Accreditation of Educator Preparation (CAEP).

Steven R. DiSalvo, PhD, seventh president of Endicott College, is a higher education leader with a track record of transformative success at multiple U.S. colleges and universities. Drawing upon his wealth of executive experience, he has stewarded major initiatives at Endicott College, including the construction of the new Cummings School of Nursing & Health Sciences academic building; a comprehensive capital campaign; a visionary strategic plan; and a commitment to diversity, equity, and inclusion, most recently demonstrated by the appointment of the college's first vice president & chief diversity officer. Notably, DiSalvo successfully led the college through a worldwide pandemic with a safe and fully open campus, record applicants and enrollments, lower debt, and a stronger endowment. Since relocating to Boston's North Shore, DiSalvo has served on the boards of the New England Council, Austin Preparatory School, Cummings Foundation, and as the chair of the Commonwealth Coast Conference. He and his wife, Eileen, are the proud parents of three adult sons, Tom, Andrew, and Connor.

Joanne McMahon, MS in ED, concluded a 45-year career in her beloved field of special education, considering herself a pioneer in a newly emerging area of education. Her work began six years prior to the enactment of the landmark legislation known as PL 94–142 (Education for All Handicapped Children Act of 1975), which ensured a free appropriate education for each child with a disability. PL 94–142 was the foundation of the current Individuals with Disabilities Education Act (IDEA of 1990). As a special education teacher, she advanced to team leader and then became the developer of a preschool intervention program for students with disabilities and later an educational administrator. She was a consultant for school districts on autism. In her supervisory role, she expanded and refined an intensive intervention program for children (ages 5–21) on the autism spectrum and provided staff development and support for general and special education teachers and staff.

Sally M. Reis, PhD, holds the Letitia Neag Chair in Educational Psychology, is a Board of Trustees Distinguished Professor, and was the former vice provost for academic affairs at the Neag School of Education at University of Connecticut. She served as principal investigator of the National Research

Center on the Gifted and Talented, department head of the educational psychology department at UConn, and president of the National Association for Gifted Children. She was a classroom teacher and administrator in public education before her work at UConn. She has authored and coauthored more than 270 articles, books, book chapters, monographs, and technical reports, and worked in a research team that has generated more than $60 million in grants in the past 15 years. Her specialized research interests are related to diverse populations of talented students, education of students with both talents and disabilities, gifted girls and women, and using enrichment and strength-based pedagogy to enhance education for all students. She has won multiple awards, including being named a UConn Board of Trustees Distinguished Professor and a fellow of Division 15 of the American Psychological Association.

Marsha Sobel grew up in Queens, New York, and attended public schools there from kindergarten through grade 12. As a child, she always loved education and reading. She would "hold school" on her outdoor steps with her sisters and neighbors as her students. She started her professional career in the New York City school system as a substitute teacher and then was assigned to one of the districts in the Bronx. When she and her family moved to the Mid-Hudson Valley, she returned to teaching in the Newburgh Enlarged City School District as a teacher (holding several different specialist positions), then elementary principal, and retired as assistant superintendent of curriculum and instruction.

Peggy Stewart, MA, is an international professional learning facilitator and leadership partner. Peggy supports districts and organizations in implementing teacher leadership systems and coaches teachers and principals in developing leadership skills. Peggy served on the consortium for the development of the teacher leader model standards and co-led development of the teacher leadership courses for the National Network of State Teachers of the Year. She currently facilitates those courses for educators in Asia, Europe, and the Americas. Peggy was a national board-certified high-school social studies teacher and was the 2005 New Jersey State Teacher of the Year. She currently serves on the board of directors for Learning Forward NJ.

www.ingramcontent.com/pod-product-compliance
Lightning Source LLC
Chambersburg PA
CBHW020741230426
43665CB00009B/513